SELLING
IN A NEW
MARKET SPACE

Getting Customers to Buy Your Innovative
and Disruptive Products

BRIAN G. BURNS and TOM U. SNYDER

New York   Chicago   San Francisco   Lisbon   London
Madrid   Mexico City   Milan   New Delhi   San Juan
Seoul   Singapore   Sydney   Toronto

The McGraw·Hill Companies

1 2 3 4 5 6 7 8 9 0   DOC/DOC   0 1 0 9

ISBN   978–0–07–163610–0
MHID   0–07–163610–2

McGraw-Hill books are available at special quantity discounts to use as premiums and sales promotions, or for use in corporate training programs. To contact a representative please visit the Contact Us pages at www.mhprofessional.com.

This book is printed on acid-free paper.

Library of Congress Cataloging-in-Publication Data
Snyder, Tom.
    Selling in a new market space : getting customers to buy your innovative and disruptive products / by Tom Snyder and Brian Burns. -- 1st ed.
        p. cm.
    ISBN 978–0–07–163610–0 (alk. paper)
1. Selling.   2. New products.   3. Technological innovations.   I. Burns, Brian, 1953- II. Title.
    HF5438.25.S648 2009
    658.85--dc22

                                                                    2009026005

Dedication

We would like to dedicate this book to all the great and diverse salespeople with whom we have had the honor of working. Special thanks to members of the Virginia Team at Rational, the Mid-Atlantic team at Object Design, Inc., the Southeastern Regional team at Rogue Wave Software, and the Public Sector team at DataPower; you have made winning both fun and exciting. A special thanks also goes to Rob Daly and Susan Burns for endless hours of feedback and support.

Contents

CONTENTS

Introduction

Anyone who has had the pleasure of being part of a new business-to-business product venture will remember both the excitement and heartache. Business-to-business products bring with them several complexities, including cost, multiple decision makers, and long sales cycles. The value of innovative and disruptive products by their own nature is difficult to communicate, making traditional marketing channels marginally valuable.

Having spent our entire careers working with early-stages companies bringing disruptive products to market, we have witnessed an obvious pattern that, as others participants have also noticed, continues to be *repeated* over and over again. The pattern begins with the big idea to *change* the rules of a market segment or the next generation of an already successful product. Regardless of how well the new venture is set up, the odds of success are slim. ***Bottom Up***

Both of our careers have focused on helping early-stage companies create and dominate their respective markets, yet we have played very different roles. Brian Burns has spent the last 20 years in sales and sales management at nine venture-backed start-ups. Burns typically was the first sales person hired and focused on capturing the initial customers. Burns' passion was not only capturing revenue but also modeling the best salespeople, and this passion evolved into a sales method that has been proven to be highly effective.

Tom Snyder has the perfect background to counterbalance Burns' experience in that his career has been focused on applying proven selling methodologies. Snyder has worked with hundreds of companies to optimize their sales model by diagnosing problems and creating unique strategies to out-compete more established players. Both of the authors had come to the same conclusions from very different perspectives: Existing sales methods were insufficient to match the challenges of selling innovative and disruptive products.

Sometimes the product and market make an excellent match and are perfectly timed for each other. Since most of the innovative world doesn't have the luxury of perfect timing, strategy, adoption, and execution, we have written this book to guide the entrepreneur who enjoys having a great team, sufficient funding, the disruptive idea, and the drive and willingness work hard.

With the explosion of new technologies, the availability of venture capital, and the excitement of entrepreneurship, there has been no shortage of new products coming to market. Even when the new company is founded by proven experts, with a game-changing innovation, backed by A-level venture capital, managed by Ivy League–educated leaders, and possessing a well-thought-out business plan, the odds of success are still stacked against them. Once Everything is in order, and the product is ready to launch. The industry analysts all predict that this new innovation is one to watch. The management team prepares the go-to-market strategy; hours are spent in their "war room" designing the PowerPoint presentation that will become the corporate standard. Each word, picture, and even the fonts of the presentation are argued over for hours, and in the end, all 75 slides are polished to perfection. The strategy is flawless, and anticipation is high.

The sales team is recruited from adjacent market leaders, all thoroughly screened and their references checked. This team is composed of experienced and the best overall performers in the industry. All of the salespeople hired have been overachievers at their previous companies and fit into the A-player profile. The stakes are too high to hire anyone who has not proven him- or herself. A kickoff meeting is scheduled; the team is assembled for training. The vision for the company is shared with the new sales team; some concerns are felt but not spoken. The sales teams learn the company pitch, and they practice and deliver it, believing they are ready to hit the ground running.

THE REALITY FOR SALES

Back in the field the salespeople feel off balance. The positive energy that was built at home office during the kickoff has waned, being replaced with doubt. The doubt is created when the sellers try to communicate the value of their new product to their targeted prospects. The company pitch, all 75 slides of gold, does not seem to build interest. In some cases the prospect does show interest for the concept and even gets excited during the demonstration of the product, but follow-up calls go unanswered. The new salespeople are in a sense fish out of water; they are used to meeting with people who already understand the value of the company's product and are willing to take meetings when requested. The sellers are used to selling additional products to people who have purchased from them in the past. They miss getting leads and having the corporate infrastructure that existed at their previous companies. They miss being treated as superstar producers and now have to deal with people questioning their judgment or even their skills. Now the sellers are not getting many meetings and the ones that they do get are not progressing to the next stage. The sellers spend their days talking with each other and coming up with a complete list of internal villains that have caused this predicament. At the top of the list are the usual suspects—marketing and product development.

When the salespeople share their experiences with each other, they notice that they are getting the same results. They reassure themselves that since they have been successful at other companies, the problem could not possibly be them. The salespeople review and practice the product positioning, presentation, and value proposition, but still they are not getting anything positive back. They call all the people in their network and meet for coffee, lunch, and cocktails. Everyone connects with their excitement, but still nothing sticks. The salespeople have convinced themselves that the problem is with how the company is not matching what the market wants and not communicating what they do clearly enough to attract qualified leads. Sure, everyone is logically right, and everyone is also culpable for not solving the real problems.

Meanwhile back at the home office, concerns are being raised that the deals on the forecast are not progressing. Management notices that the morale of the sales team has gone from positive to neutral at best. The vice president of sales assures everyone that it will just take a little more time, and then it will become so much easier. The VP of sales, of course, came from a very successful company that could not hire salespeople fast enough to keep up with demand, so he knows how to manage growth and to maximize an opportunity. The VP also feels he has his own personal magical formula that, once implemented, will replicate the same results. The CEO, concerned that revenue is taking longer than expected and that the few deals that do happen are hard-fought, reassures the management and the board that this is still a once-in-a-lifetime opportunity.

Well, little improves over time. Several quarters go by with marginal progress. The VP of sales, backing his team, pushes for the product changes that are requested by prospective clients, and some are included. Marketing takes a beating for not having a clear message and providing few leads. Marketing quickly responds with events that gather thousands of contacts that are registered as qualified leads. Within short order, the management team is circling the wagons to protect their turf, and the obvious true villain has to be the sales organization. The visionary entrepreneur is feeling like his vision is being clouded, the product development team feels that the salespeople just don't get it, and marketing feels the salespeople are lazy and are not following up on the large amount of leads they have provided. The VP of sales must take swift corrective action before it is too late. So the VP of sales lets go a couple of the weakest players or the ones that were complaining the most. The message is clear: Hiring mistakes are not avoidable but need to be corrected quickly.

Soon the replacement salespeople are selected based on the new improved profile that the VP of sales has selected, which may be one of several things, from "team player" to "hunter" or "killer." More time is bought, but the CEO is becoming concerned that the sales leadership is not strong enough, and he starts a confidential search to find someone who can "make it happen." The villain in the management team's minds has to be the VP of sales. The VP of engineering knows that they have built the best product, and his team has worked nights and weekends to ensure that. The VP of marketing has given sales more leads than they could possibly want, and there is still so little closed business. The CFO watches the big salaries and expenses go out the window with so little coming in. It is clear it is time for a change.

The few customers that are acquired are the classic early adopters, the people who are excited by the next big thing and make purchases for personal interest and not as corporate-wide standards. The early adopters are helpful because they represent revenue and corporate icons to be included on the Web site, but their strategic value is nil. The mission of the organization was not to have their product purchased only for experimentation; it was to be accepted by the enterprise and deployed throughout the enterprise. It is at this point that the mismatch of current strategy and actions needed are the furthest apart. The answer to this problem can rarely be solved by either product development or by marketing; it can only be solved by sales.

Within 18 months, all but a handful of the sales team are replaced or put on a "get well plan." The CEO digs into the sales that do happen so that he can learn what is working and why companies are purchasing the product. When the CEO meets with the few sales survivors, he is dismayed at the fact that these salespeople have not been using the standard presentation and have not been following the mandated selling process. The process that these salespeople follow is their own, and they have become successful in spite of the company, not because of it.

We label these salespeople mavericks because it is the most accurate description of the style and behavior required to sell innovative and disruptive products. In these yet-to-be-established markets being an A-level salesperson is not enough. Hard work, a positive attitude, and solid selling skills will help but will not establish sales in this new market. Selling innovations necessitates the creation of new markets, which requires a new class of salesperson that breaks classic profiles. The individuals who encompass the characteristics of awareness, appetite for risk, and an uncommon natural ability to listen and align the needs heard back to the innovation to be sold are extremely hard to identify and even harder to retain.

MAVERICKS SELLING IN A NEW MARKET

The maverick salespeople don't appear as stereotypical salespeople. Their main attribute is the ability to sell products that no one else can by creating markets that never before existed. These very successful salespeople are usually overlooked for the exact reason that makes them successful: They are being successful because they are doing what works versus what the company has mandated. This dichotomy is engendered because the people who have created the mandates are almost always not the ones with any experience selling the product. Without these maverick sellers, the years of product development and sweat equity, as well as the tens of millions of capital dollars, often go to waste. The value that the maverick sellers bring to the organization is irreplaceable. Regardless of the management challenges the maverick seller can create the market without them the innovation will just be a great idea whose time was just not right.

Several things need to be done differently by any organization that wants to create a new market and must be embraced by the organization in its entirety, not just the sales organization. The product team needs to be more responsive to what the market needs, marketing needs to be more concerned about quality versus quantity of the leads it produces, and the whole management team needs to remember if no one buys the product the company has no value—particularly the management team.

All the problems cited in the preceding scenario are large enough on their own to take a book to explore how to best solve them and are outside the scope of this book. We will focus on the selling side of the problem and share what we have seen work in a repeatable and predictable manner over a 20-year period. We will refer to the previous scenario as the conventional method of selling innovations. In contrast, we will describe in this book a method that we refer to as the maverick method. Since it is easier to learn something new by comparing it to something that is already known, we will note what makes the maverick method distinctive and compelling, and, ultimately, how to make it operational.

The conventional method is applied because it is known, understood, and generally accepted. Not applying the conventional method would be the obvious risky move, yet when it comes to innovations, the conventional method does not match the environment's obstacles and requirements of creating the market. Employing the conventional method to this environment ensures deterioration, and the response is to expand the conventional method rather than examine or replace the process that caused the deterioration. While Einstein's definition of insanity (doing the same thing over and over again and expecting different results) is often cited, it's rarely applied to sales. This forces the maverick method to be adopted at the grass roots or in stealth mode, accepted gradually and only acknowledged once it has been proven. Far too often, by the time the tide has changed, it is too late, some other company has capitalized on the opportunity or the market fails to develop into anything more than a niche.

Table I.1 The Conventional Method of Sales vs. the Maverick Method

Conventional Method	Maverick Method
Model the industry norm.	Create a model that matches what the customer needs and wants.
Sales implements the go-to-market strategy.	Sales creates the market.
Salespeople are hired from the industry leader.	Salespeople are hired from other early-stage winners.
Model is seen as the safe strategy	Model is seen as radical and unproven.
Strategy depends on the product and marketing.	Strategy depends on the sales organization.
Method is the same as their competitor's.	Method is completely different than the competitors.
Sales is responsible for revenue.	The company as a whole is responsible for revenue.

SALES TRAINING CASE STUDY

Some years ago, one of the authors was selling for a disruptive software company named Object Design, Inc., which was the *INC Magazine* number one fastest-growing company in 1994. It was an object database company run by one of the original Oracle VPs named Ken Marshall. Corporate transferred a salesperson from the home office down to Washington, D.C., to run the Mid-Atlantic commercial territory.

The salesperson had been the strategic selling trainer for the company and very successful managing inside sales for one of the most established territories. The salesperson moved to Rockville, Maryland, and sat in an office across the hall, where overhearing conversations could not be avoided. The salesperson spent a year there, struggling and frustrated, applying the skills taught in the most widely accepted sales training methodology of the time. Unfortunately, however, he did not sell a single thing. The Federal business, on the other side of the hall, however, had picked up for the federal territory—even though this was during the Clinton administration and not a lot of federal money was being spent on innovative technologies. The federal salesperson had gotten a lot of deals into the intelligence arena selling object databases for geospatial data and keeping track of images associated with disparate data.

The relocated salesperson had all these nice Miller Heiman Blue Sheets. His manager would come down from Burlington, Massachusetts, and they would go through all the Blue Sheets, smile at each other, and put some red flags up. But still nothing was sold. The company had such confidence in this senior salesperson, however, that they finally recalled him to the home office, firmly convinced that the territory was barren and that there was no business to be had in the Mid-Atlantic commercial region.

Here was a person highly trained in the skills and strategies of conventional selling, at least as they pertain to creating documents on how to make a sale. And he believed in it; he taught it. And by the way, it was great stuff. But he didn't sell a thing. Had he been in an established market, he would have done phenomenally well—because the path to success would have already been carved. The problem was that the salesperson wasn't a maverick. Mavericks don't just follow an established path; they blaze their own trails when they recognize there isn't an established one.

Over a 20-year period, we have identified the skills, strategy, and process that make up the maverick seller and what separates him or her from the rest of the pack. We see a compelling need for this book because what we have seen is the same errors being repeated over and over again. Shockingly, each organization believes that they are the first to experience these challenges, all without understanding their cause and effect.

The other observation that has repeated itself over and over again is that there is no established sales process or training that addresses these advanced skills that are needed to create and capture early-stage markets. Sales training, and the hundreds of books have been written about selling, for the most part are focused on two major types of sales: first, the interpersonal sale, or simple sale, and, second, the complex sale, which encompasses sales that involve several buying influences. In the business-to-business market, all sales fall into the complex category because they require multiple decision makers and often expand to incorporate the successful selling of innovative and disruptive products. So often we see well-established sales training classes and models applied to this most challenging environment with the same lackluster results. It is our own observation of the lackluster results of existing sales training that motivated us to research and document the missing knowledge, skills, and strategies. We have unraveled how the complex sale really works, not only the steps but the actual process that happens within the buying company. With the complete understanding of the complex sale, we have developed new selling skills and strategies that give the seller control over the buying process rather than simply reacting to it. With that being said, we are confident that by reading this book and applying the maverick skills and strategies, you will be able to create a repeatable and predictable process.

Chapter 1

Selling in a New Market Space

In 1989 IBM signed a purchase order with Rational Software Corp. for $2.5 million. The next year IBM invested $25 million in Rational, and 13 years later IBM bought Rational outright for $2.1 billion. And it all began with one Paul Levy, maverick. We're going to call what Paul Levy did an example of what is required to sell in a new market space.

THE STORY OF A MAVERICK: PAUL LEVY

Paul Levy and Mike Devlin founded Rational Machines in 1981. By 1989 they were in what has been called the *chasm*,[1] that precarious space between the visionary early adopters of disruptive new technologies and the early majority of the mainstream market. It is a time in business akin to the time when a hermit crab leaves its shell and scurries about looking for a new home—and it is a period fraught with danger. Rational was having a difficult quarter; it was running low on cash and needed a big win to raise additional venture capital.

On a sultry summer day, the two founders of Rational flew to Washington, D.C., for a meeting with the president of IBM Federal Systems. They had been given 30 minutes, at 10 a.m., on the last day of the quarter. Much rode on the outcome of that meeting. At the time, IBM Federal Systems was running the air traffic control systems at the nation's 170 major airport terminals.[2] They met in a large office and were uncomfortably nervous. A lot was at stake. After they had given the pitch, the president turned to the IBM project manager, Susan Murphy, and said, "Is this the right thing for us to do?" After a moment Ms. Murphy said, "No. Because we don't really use it enough; it's not IBM equipment; it's not running our software . . . ."

Everyone turned white. After a moment of shock, Paul Levy asked one question, "May I ask? What do you see as your largest risk with regards to meeting your projects schedule?" Ebker's answer flowed with little need to reflect: "My largest risk to meeting the schedule is being able to write all the software that is required for the project." Playing into Levy's hand, Levy rallied and started explaining his vision for revolutionizing software across the federal government, and across the world. He went into a 45-minute unbridled presentation about how the entire world economy was going to be totally dependent on software within the next decade. And as it turned out, he was right.

Paul Levy began talking, and others tried to shut the meeting down, but no one left. No one got up. It was too riveting. He started by saying that over the next five years, IBM was going to need tens of millions of dollars of Rational's products to meet productivity required to hit their commitments. He then went on to point out that he had met with the leaders of the FAA, who realized that this project was critical to the United States' air traffic control system and to the safety of each passenger. As he built the vision, it expanded beyond IBM, the project, and even the nation.

By the end, it was a new vision for the world. And by 5:30 p.m., they walked out with a $2.5 million purchase order in hand.

Levy just wouldn't let them leave. They needed to understand the Big Picture. Most sellers would have quit at the words of Susan Murphy: "I'm sorry. We just don't need what you have to offer." They'd sheepishly say, "OK, well, thanks anyway." And then they'd go back to their manager and say, "They didn't like it." And that would be the end of the story. But Paul Levy was no ordinary salesperson. He was a maverick, a salesperson par excellence.

What made Paul Levy unusual was that he was both so inherently passionate about his vision and frustrated that no one saw it that he was going to share his vision and they were literally going to have to leave him in mid-sentence if they didn't want to listen. It has been said that where there is no vision, the people perish. The unstated corollary is that where there is vision, the people flourish. Levy understood the importance of the vision, and he realized that he *had* to express it, to make the full reality of the need apparent and the power of the outcome evident. He understood that Ms. Murphy was too narrowly focused, too myopic to see the magnificence of the vision. He needed to back up and paint the picture of what the future could look like. And on that basis, he ended up with a $2.5 million purchase order on the last day of the quarter, at a time when the company was in desperate need of it.

BY DEFINITION, A MAVERICK

It must be said at the outset that "the maverick method" may be a bit of a misnomer—even an oxymoron, because mavericks by definition do not stick to the prescribed formula. It is more of an "approach." Every salesperson may have a unique approach, but there are characteristics and skills that are common to them all. These teachable skills can be developed into an art.

WordNet 3.0 defines a *maverick* as "someone who exhibits great independence in thought and action"[3]—and such is the sense in which we shall use it. It is the salesperson who is ideally suited to sell innovations or disruptive technologies in new, untested markets. It is the salesperson who successfully sells new products in new markets (see Figure 1.1). It is the sales person who goes outside the predetermined boundaries. It is the salesperson who gets things done. This book is not about the left half of the matrix in this figure—that is, we are not concerning ourselves with *existing* products, either with new or existing customers (although the skills and techniques that we will be describing are applicable to any selling situation). We are looking at *new* products, sometimes with existing customers but

Products

	Existing	New
New	**Customer acquisition**	**New market growth**
Customers		
Existing	**Customer penetration**	**New product introduction**

Figure 1.1 Existing versus new customer and product matrix.

19

mostly with new customers: the new market quadrant at the top right of the matrix.

New products in existing markets (new product introduction) and new products in new markets (new market growth) require highly skilled salespeople. The new market quadrant is not for the novice. Selling in this quadrant requires the salesperson to create markets from scratch. You don't get a handicap—these markets do not previously exist. Creating a new market requires developed skills at pinpointing potential pockets of interest, developing and building that interest, and creating real value for the potentially interested parties. There is no sense in employing a novice, or even the B-team, to do this. They simply won't have the experience or the skill to execute.

But before we leave the subject of definitions, let's take care of a few that will help in our discussion. First, maverick salespeople deal in the world of the complex sale—that is, in a world where the marketing strategy merely plays a supporting role. It does not drive the sale; it doesn't make the complex sale. That is the responsibility of the sales organization. It is simply too complex for marketing to handle. The complex sale has a long sales cycle (taking several calls to close); it requires a large commitment by the buyer (and the consequences matter); it has more than one decision maker; and it often involves a long-term relationship between the companies.

Next, let's define *innovation* and *disruptive technology*. We will often use the terms in tandem, but they are not interchangeable and they do not refer to the same things. Innovations can be *any* products or services, in *any* industry, that are new, often paradigm-changing, and disruptive to the status quo. They usually portend some kind of a learning curve for the user, and most of the time there is no ready-made market for them. Like the innovative product or service itself, the market must be created from ground zero. We are not talking about marginal, or even terrific, improvements to existing products or services. We are talking about what is genuinely fresh, original, and perhaps unprecedented.

The term *disruptive technology* was coined by Joseph L. Bower and Clayton M. Christensen in their January 1, 1995, *Harvard Business Review* article "Disruptive Technologies: Catching the Wave." Disruptive technology describes a technological innovation, product, or service that uses a "disruptive"[4] strategy, rather than a "revolutionary"[5] or "sustaining"[6] strategy, to overturn the existing dominant technologies or status quo products in a market. It disrupts the marketplace by being newer, cheaper, faster—and usually not until later—better.

START WITH A VISION

Let's return for a moment to Rational Software and look at some of the elements of selling in a new market space. The first lesson we learned is that with innovation, it is vital that you create the vision for the customer. Create a vision for the future; for the benefits that your product or service will bring. Paul Levy painted a picture of a whole world running on software; he wove a tapestry so grand and immense that it couldn't be forgotten and compelled IBM to buy his vision on the spot.

Vision is crucially important in the new market sale because the sale takes place very early. So early, in fact, that the customer usually doesn't even know he or she is in the market for something new. Everything is humming along quite nicely in the customer's domain, and there may be no hint of trouble on the horizon. So when you're selling innovation, you're selling in an earlier phase of the decision cycle of your customers that most sellers have never faced before—hence the need to create vision, a vision of a different kind of world.

Late in 1989, the salespeople at Rational hit a wall. It was a strong group of salespeople, many of them from Hewlett-Packard, an established major player in the high-tech industry. They were bright and energetic and had been very successful in conventional sales. But they were facing a new challenge. They were being asked to sell a powerful computer and accompanying software, internally referred to as a "Box," for a million dollars. All they had to do, or so it seemed to them, was sell the box and then reap the rewards. That's the way it had worked at Hewlett-Packard: The customer bought the box; they knew how to use it; they used it to maximum capacity; and then they bought more. Simple, right? But there was a missing link between the vision and the reality. Missing in the sense that it didn't exist—at least not yet. The problem was that these excellent conventional salespeople would sell a box, mainly to large defense contractors. These contractors would buy the box, and it would sit in their data center and never get used. They were certainly not in the market for repeat business with Rational, because the dream never came alive for them. Sales fell off quickly. The model didn't scale. Something radical had to be done.

It is a hallmark of the new market salesperson that he or she plows new ground, independent of what would normally be expected of the salesperson. The salesperson does something that at the time seems rather radical, even crazy, but in hindsight it turns out to be completely obvious.

The reason sales had fallen off was because customers simply weren't using the product. It was too different than what they were used to, and no one had taken the time to integrate it with their existing software development systems. The customer's perception of the risk involved far outweighed the desire to harvest the promised benefits. When you're selling new products to new customers, which is what the Rational salespeople were doing, then one of the most important things is to have ease of implementation. Customers' perception of risk is very high. Their perception of risk prevents them from engaging the technology without a safety net. The answer, of course, is to mitigate the risk and provide the safety net.

When you hire the A-players from the adjacent leaders to sell into a new market, they're coming from a world where implementation is always well understood and relatively easy because it's an established offering. It's something customers are familiar with; they've used it multiple times. The customer is very well-informed, and he or she knows as much as the seller does about implementing it. When a seller grows up in that world and comes to the new market world, the seller doesn't perceive that the customer sees only risk.

At Rational, it was John Lovett, the VP of North American Sales, and one of the Washington, D.C.–based sales teams who cracked the code. Lovett was the sales leader, and he had noticed that one of his teams was over achieving, apparently by investing a substantial amount of time with each customer *after* the initial sale. That sales team realized that to get repeat sales, customers would not only have to use the product, but they'd have to maximize its capacity to receive the intended benefits. Lovett figured out that customers weren't using the product because the implementation was perceived as too complex and simply too much for the customer to figure out. He decided to change the sales model. Completely. Realizing that customers would be unlikely to pay more for implementation assistance, he decided to offer it for free if the customers were not willing to pay for it. He realized that his team needed to integrate the product into the customers' environment and then teach them how to use it, reducing the resistance to adapting the approach.

Rational changed from selling boxes to selling an application environment that helped customers automate their development, accelerating the productivity of the software engineering teams. And it wasn't just a lone salesperson anymore. It was a salesperson and a whole team of engineers. They would go into an account, teach the people how to use the product, and integrate the product with the customers' existing environment. At last, customers were getting the full benefit of the product. The engineers didn't cost a dime. It was their job to ensure that the product be used, and that the customer be satisfied. It was radical, and it was completely unconventional, but it worked. It was the catalyst for change that took Rational from $10 million in sales to $25 million in one year, creating a repeatable and predictable sales method. And after 20 years and after IBM acquired Rational, the model is still in use to this day.

Rational is a classic example of selling into a market space. Paul Levy sold the vision; John Lovett found a way to implement it. His way was considered risky and radical at the time—but he was proven right.

Another example of the successful use of the maverick method is the company that recently sold a new security system to Harrods Casino. It was a great and disruptive purchase by the casino, and genuinely risky. In order to mitigate the risk, the maverick CEO of the security company sat an engineer outside the door of the Harrods Casino CEO. He was promised to Harrods for 120 days. And he just sat there reading magazines, until there was a problem. As soon as anything went wrong, the CEO had merely to poke his nose into the hall and the engineer (who had immediate access to anyone he needed at the home office) was there to fix the problem. It provided a comfort level because the risk has been reduced greatly. And as a result, the inevitable implementation gaffes were minimal and troubleshooting was immediate. Everything turned up roses on what might otherwise have been a disaster.

There's a funny story that illustrates the notion of the disconnect between vision and implementation. Charles Atlas (the Arnold Schwarzenegger of his day) sold the dream of all young lads: the perfect body. Many of you will remember the famous advertisement that appeared on the back of comic books—that advertisement caught the attention of one young boy in particular.

Charles Atlas told the story about getting a letter from this young boy, which read:

> Dear Mr. Atlas,
>   I sent you my 50 cents and I received your pamphlet. Thank you very much. When can I expect my muscles?

Amusing, and yet it perfectly illustrates what had happened at Rational: Paul Levy successfully sold a magnificent vision, but there was nobody delivering on that vision. Levy had made a leap from saying it's a box that gives you a set of benefits, but missing in the middle was the hard part.

The sellers thought it an easy sell: This box produces those benefits. They gave stellar presentations, all vision and possibilities. Because of their relationship with the customer, or trust or what have you, some customers said, "OK, I'll give you a million dollars for the box." It sounds almost farcical, but it actually happened. Levy got his sales force to believe that his box delivered the vision, when in fact the box only enabled the vision. The only way to deliver the vision was to link up the box and the vision with a group of people who did the implementation. And that implementation had to include training, integration, and whatever else was necessary to raise the comfort level of customers and get them to use the million-dollar box.

It should also be said that these new markets were selling into a space where neither the seller nor the customer had any experience with making it work; hence the need to focus on implementation—which is about making it work. You connect whatever it is you're selling and the vision with a bridge called

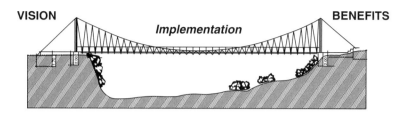

Figure 1.2 Bridging vision to benefits.

"implementation." It's plowing new ground for both seller and buyer, so it takes overinvestment of resources on the part of the seller.

As shown in Figure 1.2, the implementation itself is part of the sales process, not the purchase. That's why Rational gave it away for free. The implementation has been the missing link in the selling process of new products into a new market space. The reasons why the implementation is overlooked are many. Most likely the cause is created by organization's leadership coming from established markets, where the implementation is both understood and anticipated. Of course, in the ideal world, the implementation would be best handled by making the product simple enough that anyone can implement it, but the nature of new products is that they are complex and all the contingencies are not yet identified.

In sales we are directed to go out and get the next big deal, but without references and repeat business from existing customers, the next big deal becomes no easier than the last big deal. So the success of the implementation must become as important as the closure of the next big deal if the seller and company have any chance at winning their new market.

Chapter 2

The Innovative
and Disruptive
Market Space

The innovative and disruptive market space is the most challenging and least understood market space. Selling into a new market space is by far the most difficult for several reasons. First, the seller must understand how new markets naturally evolve. Second, the seller must understand how new markets can be created by reducing the resistance to adoption and increasing the perceived value of your product.

To describe the innovative and disruptive market space, we have found the matrix in Figure 2.1 to be both simple and powerful. The matrix focuses on two characteristics of the deal. The top shows the value to the seller, and the left-hand side shows the resistance in selling. The value to the seller is both perceived and actual, and basically reflects how much better business will be once he or she acquires this customer.

All customers are not equal, and how they use the product will vary. Further questions will arise, such as whether they could be a reference or whether there will be repeat business. The answers to these questions will contribute to the value of the opportunity beyond just the revenue. Take, for example, the subprime mortgage market of the 2000s. These mortgages proved low-resistance because the loan officers were just making the application information up and the value of the mortgages turned out to be

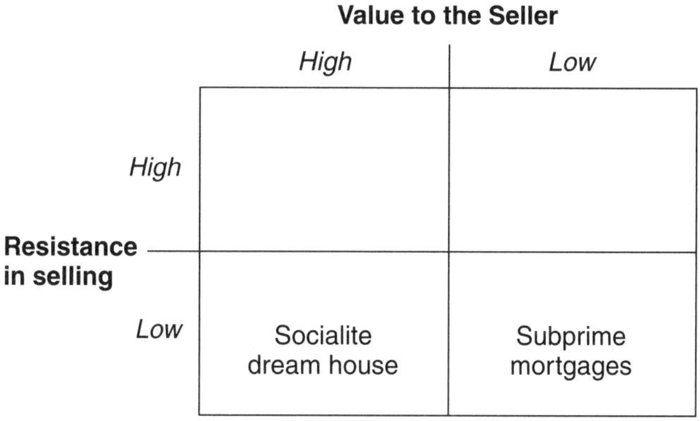

Value to the Seller

	High	Low
High		
Low	Socialite dream house	Subprime mortgages

Resistance in selling

Figure 2.1 The value and resistance matrix.

lower than low. The opposite would be the wealthy socialite who is building a dream house that will provide high visibility and the opportunity to serve friends within the socialite's network. So the resistance is low because the socialite is well off, and the value is high because there is follow-on business through the circle of friends.

The resistance in selling is a much more complex topic because it completely depends on whom you are asking. If you are asking a salesperson, he or she may say it is extremely hard because there are no leads and the product does not work. If you ask the CEO, he or she will say that it is simple because this product will change the way business is done and anyone who does not get it will miss out. It is the perception of this resistance that will impact the organization's ability to capture a new market. Far too often the perception is that the resistance is caused by everyone in the organization except the individual who is talking; this finger-pointing wastes a critical amount of time and becomes the mantra of the failing players. It will be the organization that removes the most amount of resistance that will win this new market.

The resistance can come from all parts of the organization. The product can be complex and hard to use, it can be fragile and break easily, or it can just be overpriced. Regardless of the amount of resistance, it is still up to the salespeople to sell the innovative product and get as much money as possible for it. It is up to sales to find a way to reduce the resistance and bridge the company to the customer. This bridging responsibility is rarely done and sometimes not even considered. The conventional view is that the sales organization "should just sell what we have," and the sales organization believes that their company "does not get it." Without some maverick-like catalyst, the company will blow in the winds of the market, having its destiny determined by market forces and not its own potential.

TARGET USE OF THE PRODUCT

Lowest-resistance and highest-value use of the product is the best target for the new market. It may appear obvious, but too often the sellers spend time in the wrong quadrant and ignore the inevitable results. People often feel most comfortable selling into the low-resistance/low-value prospects because they are easier and quicker. The reason you do not want to spend much time in the low-resistance/low-value space is that you will not be able to make your sales quota, and these deals will distract you from creating the real market that you will need in order to dominate in this market space.

As shown in Figure 2.2, most CEOs and the VPs of sales want to go directly to the highest-value prospects regardless of the resistance level because these are the high-profile accounts and the CEO/VP of sales are the ones that do not feel the resistance. The conflict is all but unavoidable because of the different vantage points of the executives and their inexperience at creating new markets. Marketing may target the higher-value players, but what they attract are the low-value/low-resistance leads, and it is these low-value leads with which the sales team works. It is the salespeople who have to fight the battles regardless of the internal conflicts and being misdirected. This inconsistency and fragmented view of exactly what is the target market demands an unconventional salesperson. The salespeople need to have their own compass to guide them to the best targets and not be distracted by the directives of those above them.

The more accepted and traditional way to look at selling into a new market space is to view the technology adoption curve.

| | | **Value to the Seller** | |
		High	*Low*
Resistance in Selling	*High*	CEO/VP of sales	
	Low	Target market	Marketing and most salespeople

Figure 2.2 The value and resistance matrix with the targets filled in.

The curve is a macro view of the market and is helpful to understand the process that the market will take to accept a new innovation. From a selling standpoint, each deal is very different, and yes, a prospect can fit into one of the segments. However, the value/resistance matrix is much more focused because it describes the dynamics that are actually going to determine the likelihood of a purchase.

Everett Rogers applied a bell-shaped curve to show the adoption of technology, starting with the innovators and ending with laggards. This is a well-accepted way to represent the profiles of who will buy and when. The value/resistance matrix is another way to represent the adoption by adding a "why they will buy" factor. In the complex sale, the labels have to do with a company or origination, which makes selling even more complex because you can have a laggard organization and an individual who is an innovator. Figure 2.3 shows each of the adoption stages mapped into the value/resistance matrix. This is helpful because it can

Value to the Prospect

		High	Low
Resistance in Implementing	*High*	**Early majority**	**Laggard**
	Low	**Early adopters**	**Innovators**

Figure 2.3 The value and resistance matrix completed with the market adoption stages.

become the communications tool the different groups within the organization use to determine what deals and markets to target.

In 1991 Geoffrey Moore's *Crossing the Chasm* expanded on Roger's work by stating that there is a chasm, or stalling point, that is reached at the early-adopter stage. These chasms are created by exhausting the number of buyers at the current segment and not having the product or distribution channels that are needed to capture the buyers at the next segment. We agree that there is this a chasm, but where we differ is in the belief of how to get beyond it. In the consumer or simple sale, it is clearly up to marketing and product development to create the strategy and execute against it. In the complex sale, however, it is the sales organization that is best equipped to define and execute the winning strategy.

What is different about the complex sale that makes the sales organization better equipped to create the winning strategy? Just think who actually meets with prospects and customers. Who hears the compliments and the complaints? Who has the majority of their income based on the success of capturing the early-majority buyers?

So why is sales not defining the strategy? Several reasons are ubiquitous. First, sales is seen as the executors of the corporate strategy, not the creators of it. The VP of sales is typically the last key executive to be hired and the first to be replaced. He or she is the liaison between the market and the executive committee, and is the only one who has a quantitative way to be judged on a quarterly base. The law of proximity will apply. The VP of sales that is out in the field working on deals will not be at the home office, and that means that he or she will not be included in several side discussions that involve the direction of the organization. If the VP of sales focuses on the home office politics, he or she will not be included in the key deals that are taking place and will miss out on the key issues that clients are sharing. So the go-to-market strategy is defined by those who rarely meet a customer and never fight a competitor. The analysis of sales results is being judged by those who were not involved in the deal and may have never been involved in a deal. The strategy to lower resistance and increase value is being determined at the headquarters by executives that base their approach on their own personal wins and are rarely based on the realities of the market space.

Now let's look at how each of the categories behave and the issues associated with selling to them.

INNOVATORS

The first people to embrace a new product will be those who are turned on by innovation and newness. These are people who are predisposed to different ways of solving current problem or are even looking for a problem to solve. You may ask yourself, if the innovators are so easy and may even seek you out, why not focus exclusively on them? The problem with innovators is that their job is typically not in the core of the organization for which they work. The innovators will take all your time and even sell you on how great things will be if you can get them to use your product. You can qualify the innovators quickly; they ask lots of well-researched questions and may even know more about your products than you do. The innovators will do detailed evaluations. They will be very interested in how your product was implemented or manufactured, and they appear very creditable and influential. The problem with the innovators is that they have very little budget and are masters at manipulating salespeople.

The junior salesperson who is happy to have anyone to meet with, never mind show great interest, will spend enormous amounts of time with the innovator, comfortable in the belief that anyone who spends this much time on his or her product will be spending big. The shallow qualification questions are answered with a self-serving, grandiose vision of enterprise-wide deals that are initiated once the innovator is satisfied. Most of the time, the innovator is not doing this out of malice but rather because of their own overestimated sense of self-value.

Innovators are passionate about new and better ways and have sold their company on their ideas enough to justify their position, which can be completely focused on investigating new alternatives. The innovator's business is useful and valuable in the sense that they can spend some money, and when satisfied, they will be advocates. Selling to innovators is simple yet frustrating. Innovators are very responsive to marketing because they proactively search out new products, attend trade shows, and study industry periodicals.

Winning over the innovators is very powerful, but it is just the start. These early wins need to be exploited as evidence that your product is the leader and to explain how you were selected over your competition. Years later a couple of these innovators' dreams will come true, and enterprise-wide change will take place. However, the innovative segment is not enough to sustain a company because without building on these successes and leveraging them into the early adopter, your product will die a quick death.

THE EARLY ADOPTER

The difference between the innovator and the early adopter is that the early adopter has a tangible and immediate business problem that needs solving. How to sell to early adopters is very different because they are not looking for new, exciting products. They only care about improving their business. The early adopters are visionaries—not about products but rather business results.

The reason a chasm is created between the innovators and the early adopters is that in the business-to-business space, the sale becomes exponentially more complex, and new skills and strategies are needed. Marketing's value becomes only marginally effective because the early adopters is not looking for a solution and most likely does not even acknowledge that there is a problem. The pain of a business problem will be felt, but the awareness is not yet there.

THE EARLY MAJORITY

The early majority is the segment that you want to get to, and because it is in the high-resistance and high-value quadrant, it is the next logical step in the sales evolution. The failure to gain acceptance and dominate the early majority will result in being niche player struggling to stay afloat. The early majority is very different than the early adopter segment in that the vision is a distant second to the pragmatic business decision. The early majority will accept that there is now a market segment and will recognize that the most import characteristic is which company has the established leadership position.

Selling to the early majority can be characterized by one word: competition.

SIMPLE SALE DVR CASE STUDY

The DVR market was pioneered by TiVo in the late 1990s by evolving the recording of television onto a special-purpose appliance containing a computer hard drive. This is a consumer example of discontinuous innovation, replacing the now-primitive video cassette recorder (VCR). The experience of setting a recording with a VCR is universally understood by a segment of the population. The old joke "My VCR's clock blinks 12:00 because I cannot figure out how to set it" classifies the technically handicapped, or laggard. Most of us have bravely attempted scheduling a recording on a VCR and having failed for several reasons; the clock was on a.m. and not p.m., the tape was not rewound, or the channel was not set correctly.

TiVo solved all these problems and lots more; recording can be set from the guide, a wish list, even from your cell phone. TiVo did not require cassettes or a clock to be set. It was simple to use, and it even learned your preferences and recorded programs that it thought you would like. So the value of the TiVo was huge over the VCR, but what was the resistance in implementing TiVo? Well, you did need to dial out to get updated TV schedules, you had to hook it up to your existing home entertainment system, and you had to learn a new remote. The resistance was low enough for the early majority but too high for the laggards.

The laggards' resistance was later reduced by the satellite and cable companies that built DVR functionality into their appliances that solved the installation and remote issues. Even with a far inferior product, the cable and satellite companies were able to capture the market because they lowered the resistance and provided the minimum value that matched the majority of the market.

The DVR case study is helpful because most of us can relate to it and have lived through the process. The case study is also helpful to show the new market selling issues that are faced. When you are selling in the new market space, the key is reducing resistance and increasing value. As a salesperson, you may feel that reducing resistance is outside of your control, but there are several things that are inside the salesperson's circle of control. The salesperson can simplify the evaluation process, foster understanding of how the business will be better, and orchestrate the decision process. Salespeople can reduce the cost with discounting, but, unfortunately, this an overused tool.

THE IMPLEMENTATION

Implementation of an innovation or disruptive technology is the bread and butter of the maverick salesperson. The implementation is all about reducing the resistance and increasing value for the customer. It is the key to success. As we discussed previously, it is sometimes worth doing the implementation for free. Indeed, in new market selling, the implementation needs to be part of the *cost of sales*. It has to be flawless, as it may be the only chance for success. The new market seller will take full advantage of this opportunity by being absolutely certain that the implementation is flawless and absolutely certain that the customer will use that implementation. The seller will grind out as much of an endorsement as he or she can get.

THE CAUSE OF THE CHASM

The chasm is created by exhausting the pool of innovators and, more importantly, by not reducing the resistance that broadens the pool of possible customers. The sales organization needs to identify and develop the skills to sell to both the visionary early adopters and the pragmatic early majority. Each of the groups of the organization owns a piece of reducing resistance and increasing value, but, of course, it is sales team that is responsible for bridging the company to the customer. What too often happens is that the company does not realize it needs to change in order to capture the next group of buyers, who have very different reasons for buying. The innovators will not run out of requirements that the company must implement.

Marketing becomes less effective after the innovator group is on board, and when attracting the early adopters, marketing is more about arming the sales team and less about surfacing interested targets. Since early adopters are not looking, the typical marketing outlets do not get much traction. The salespeople need to find their own leads and build interest by themselves. The good news for the salespeople is that these deals are larger and will compound into additional accounts.

A COMPLEX SALE TARGET MARKET CASE STUDY

Let's take a look at the early adopter process from start to finish. Kintana, a start-up software consulting company, "productized" a visual and executable workflow engine and had raised $10 million in venture capital. They built visual workflows that basically resembled factory assembly lines, only for building software. It was all done in the Java programming language, so it could run on anything and integrate with everything. But they didn't know how to sell it. Their vision was that they'd become the centerpiece of the whole software assembly line for the enterprise. Unfortunately, no one was using it.

So they hired a small team of salespeople. One of their maverick salespeople closed a $2 million deal with U.S. Internetworking in Annapolis, Maryland, the kingpin of their market niche. It took six months from cold call to close. He got their entire software assembly line automated, which was an enormous challenge, because they were an application service provider (ASP). They hosted, for example, a Microsoft Exchange so that their clients wouldn't have to buy any hardware, hire operations people, back up the application, or anything else.

So they had to put an enormous amount of hardware servers up. A hardware server came in with no software on it; they had to install the operating system and all the applications. Anyone who has installed several different software products knows that lots can go wrong and that it is very time-consuming. Then there was development, test, staging, and production versions of the hardware. And they had to keep track of all of it—on all these servers. They purchased Kintana to automate and keep track of it all (they'd actually been doing the workflow by writing installation scripts, and it was onerous, requiring a great deal of human intervention). They had enormous amounts of pain but did not know there was a solution in the marketplace. Enter our salesperson, who worked with them to elicit an unexpressed pain and find the unanticipated solution.

It's a great case study of how you take a technology to market. You simply can't market it. Try buying an ad that says: VISUALLY EXECUTABLE WORKFLOWS!! Everyone's already has got a workflow engine, but few can make that leap from "That does what? And I need it?" to "Right, then. I'll take it!" So someone has to elicit the pain and map the pain to the product's value. Someone has to create and build the vision.

And the salesperson had to build off of what they were experiencing, which was an out-of-control manual process. Then he had to create a real-world analogy for what the Kintana product would do for the software assembly line. Our maverick had to build a bigger vision; not displace what they had, but make it bigger than what they had.

In selling new products into a new market space, it is the salesperson's responsibility to reduce the risk of change and to prove the product will add tremendous value. We will describe the process of how to do this in later chapters. In addition, we will identify both the process and give several case studies of what happens when the process is done successfully and what can go wrong if it is ignored.

Chapter 3

Creating and Building the Vision

One of the missing skills required by someone selling in the new market is the ability to discern the problem that the seller's product solves—the ability to build the pain into the vision of what is possible once the product is implemented. In the new market space the standard approach for communicating a product's value takes one of two typical patterns. The first is to describe the technical characteristics in relation to the innovators that are enamored and the product's latest technical advances, but as we have already explained, the innovation market is a good start but not the end game. The second is to align the product with the current industry trends that are themselves aligned with an established market. Neither of these two approaches will help the field salespeople capture the early adopters that will create the new market segment. Our point here is not so much that marketing does not "get it," but rather that it requires a direct sales approach and that marketing is just not going to be able to have the impact that management would expect.

Without the vision creation skill, the seller will use his or her slide show, which will put the prospect into a trance, reminding him or her not to answer the phone ever again.

The early adopters by nature are visionaries open to competitive advantage. They are willing to take measured risks but will not champion the product within their company. This type of visionary will need support, more support than most product companies envision providing. The support needs to be included as part of the sale and not a charge item, which is a leap that will separate the successful maverick seller from the also-ran.

Unfortunately, the management team, having come from established markets, is used to serving their early majority customers whom they worked hard to establish but whom now the team is milking for all they can get. The sales organization in a new market space often feels like they are working for a different company than the one presented when they are at home office. The sales team has two choices: Convince the management team that they will need to reorganize to address the needs of the early adopters, or clandestinely apply all their resources to the sales challenge. If the former were successful, this book would be deemed unnecessary.

So, what are the components of a vision?

THE COMPONENTS OF A VISION

Selling into a new market space is by definition selling into a world where the customer does not perceive the problem. The customer may feel the pain, but they don't have a label for it yet. Or maybe they don't even feel pain. When that is the case, the salesperson is selling something that the prospect does not know that they want. And they don't want it because they don't know the *vision of the possible*.

People who drove a horse and buggy didn't generally say, "What I need is an internal combustion engine that will take me faster." They were fine using a horse. They didn't travel very far, and they didn't want to go too fast. Perhaps they were uncomfortable with machines, so why change? Remember that autos were first purchased as a novelty by rich people. It was kind of like buying your own submarine. It was truly a novel thing. Automobile manufactures had to wait until people thought: "I need to go farther; I need to go faster—there's an advantage to doing that." When the Ford Motor Company reduced the economic resistance and increased the value by providing a reliable automobile, then the idea of a car made sense.

Today, the customer could be someone at a large pharmaceutical company who is very comfortable spending a billion dollars to get a drug to market, and they're very comfortable with their failure rate because it's a 60-year-old process that's been thoroughly vetted and it works. Whether the process is good or bad, or whether it's painful or not, is not really the point. Their general attitude is, "it works and has for many years, so leave me alone."

The all-important *vision creation* discussion begins with a conversation about the business, about the way the industry typically functions. And it begins with a set of questions revolving around "what is the frustration that is experienced relative to the problem your product solves?" This then evolves into mapping the current problem that the prospect is experiencing to the business impact and the desired end result.

So the first part of developing the vision is the recognition that you are talking about a problem that customers either (a) don't know exists or (b) know exists but they can't quite put their finger on it. The second part involves creating a space within which customers can reach a conclusion by connecting the dots for themselves. The more elegant sale is the one where the seller then takes all of that complexity and distills it into a single sentence or a phrase, as for example, in the Kintana case study in Chapter 2, where the key phrase software "assembly line" summed up a complete vision.

In short, creating the vision goes like this:

Step 1: Identify the problem that the customer (and the market-place) doesn't feel; what is the experience that they have not put a label on?

Step 2: Create a comparative Then and Now, a simple two- or three-sentence analogy or metaphor that is simple and easy to understand.

Step 3: Move to a set of provocative questions that build up the awareness of the current situation and the urgency to act.

Let's go through each step in more detail.

STEP 1

Step 1 is best understood by thinking about our digital video recorder example from the previous chapter. For the DVR, the first step would be to make a list of the experiences that could create pain, frustration, and inconvenience.

To make this concept simple, think about how you would apply this process to selling a friend a DVR. What is the pain that has not yet been acknowledged? First, let's take the DVR's ability to pause live TV. Now let's come up with some examples that people can relate to. Since questions are infinitely more effective than statements, you could ask your friend, "Have you ever been into a football game and all of a sudden the doorbell rings? What if you could just freeze the game just at that moment and restart it when you are ready?" Today this capability is well understood, but just a few years ago it was borderline magic.

The key situation you need to avoid in Step 1 is the "so what?" or "who needs that?" situation. This is why you need an experience-based question versus a comparison-based question. The comparison-based question focuses the prospect on how they would solve the problem with the current solution. The comparison questions typically do not elicit enough pain and often take the focus off your solution and keep the prospect stuck on the existing approach. For example, if you return to the DVR example and ask "How would you freeze live TV with a VCR?" this question would focus your friend on having a tape preloaded and hitting Record, then rewinding later. The comparison questions are the most common because they are easy to come up with, but as you can see, they are counterproductive.

During Step 1 you will also quickly be able to determine the type of person you are addressing. For instance, if you are getting a response such as, "that is not a big issue for me," one of two things is wrong, either, your question may not be eliciting a strong enough problem or the prospect is a laggard. We have all dealt with laggards before; they are stuck in their own way of doing things. Laggards are ones who still use typewriters and do not trust ATMs. So, clearly, laggards fit into the low-value/high-resistance category.

Think of all the experiences that cause pain that the DVR can solve:

- Interruption
  - Phone call
  - People talking
  - Doorbell
  - Someone walking into the room
  - Kids playing
  - Urgent matter
- Complexity with the VCR
  - Setting the clock
  - Setting the start time
  - Making sure you have a tape and that it's rewound
  - Finding more than one program on the same tape
  - Making sure that the tape is not write-protected

Once you use these scenarios to find the prospect's pain point, then you can move on to Step 2.

STEP 2

Innovative and disruptive products are usually on the cutting edge of technology, and the people who created them have very complicated ways to describe them. These complex descriptions can be good because they give the image of sophistication and power. We have a natural inclination to talk about the powerful "secret sauce" of the product, but people may not understand the characteristics and may not care. The problem quickly becomes that no one knows what you are talking about or what it means to them. Imagine, for example, talking about the DVR by describing the size of the disk or its parallel operating system; these characteristics may be interesting to innovators, but the early majority buys in order to solve problems.

What the seller has to be able to do is to convert that into a simple, comparative two- or three-sentence story that lasts no more than 30 seconds. And that story has to create an analogy with two components: the solution is similar to what his product is solving and the benefits are obvious in the story. Think about the x-raying of luggage at an airport. Regardless of what you think about the Transportation Security Administration, no one has to say "What's the benefit of x-raying my luggage?" It's faster, it's easier, and it's safer than airport security rooting through each bag. The standard corporate slide presentation is describing something that's unknown; the analogy is describing something everybody knows. It's like the software assembly line described in Chapter 2. Everybody has seen an assembly line, but no one would have imagined what a software assembly line looks like.

Let's consider an example in the business-to-business space. DataPower, developed in 1999, was first described as a "Web Services firewall." This is a perfect example of how without a clear analogy people simply do not understand what the product is and why anyone would need it. The description discussed the product's function, which was accurate yet completely worthless. Sales prospects would hear the description and think, "I already have a firewall." This caused the salespeople to think that the prospect did not "get it," and the prospect did not see any reason why the company would need it. As with most innovative and disruptive products, if you position them relative to the current generation of products, they naturally equate the new product with the current product.

What you have to do is build up an analogy that everyone can relate to and that separates the product from the current generation's solution. To sell the idea of a Web Service firewall, we used an airport analogy: "Think about what happens when you go to the airport. You pass throw several levels of security. First you get your boarding pass by identifying yourself. Next you move into the security line, which requires someone matching your identification and your boarding pass. Then your baggage must be X-rayed, and you must walk through a metal detector. The Web Services firewall is the X-ray machine. Current firewall products just check your identification, which is not enough. Who would get on a plane when all luggage has not been completely X-rayed to ensure that no weapons or explosives are carried on?" With this analogy everyone immediately understood the benefits of this firewall/X-ray machine and determined that it is a must-have because the alternative is unthinkable. The experience that is elicited is universal; everyone has flown in plane and is familiar with the consequences of not thoroughly examining each passenger.

It's a simple analogy, but very powerful. All of a sudden people get it: "Oh, you look inside, you make sure there's nothing dangerous, and anything that makes it through is OK. Great idea!" Yet it took two years of selling it to figure out that simple analogy. The salespeople would go in with the 75-slide deck in their presentation, they'd present brilliantly, and then they'd leave and the response would be "We're not sure we need this." We were able to convince customers that everybody who does Web services needs this functionality; otherwise, it would be like leaving your house unlocked. Until a maverick came up with the airport luggage x-ray analogy, the vision went largely unheeded.

STEP 3

If you're telling the analogy right, you've got two outcomes. First, people relate to it and can see the need for the product, and second, they feel what the consequences of not using your product would be. The simple analogy can transfer the value of the product without talking about feature function or making the prospect sit through a brain-numbing presentation. The analogy is also simple to remember and allows the prospect to share it with others within his or her organization.

The analogy can be expanded by asking questions that elicit the pain that will be personally experienced if the product is not purchased. In the firewall/airport analogy, the questions are simple: "Would you want to be the person who ignored the need to have an X-ray machine?" or "What would happen to you if something goes horribly wrong and management learned that it was preventable?" These questions force the prospect to experience the consequences if action is not taken. The rhetorical response is personal and emotional.

With the DVR case the questions may naturally move to the positive, for example, "How would you like it if someone could search every available television show and record the ones that match your interests?" This question elicits the possible, but pain-evoking questions are much more effective; for example, "Have you ever missed a great football game or been distracted and missed an unbelievable play?"

Having several of these questions prepared and practiced is needed to polish off the vision and reinforce the value of your product.

Building the vision is a skill that is required in the new market space and must be taken on by the individual salesperson. What we have seen is that marketing will generate elevator pitches and value propositions that include buzzwords and technical prowess but are completely void of anything that a prospect can relate to. The best vision statements are those that even a laggard can understand and relate his or her personal experience to.

Chapter 4

The Natural Laws of Selling Innovation

Whenever you really want to learn how to be great at a particular profession, you must first understand the guiding principles or laws of that vocation. Regardless of whether or not a person acknowledges the truth, sales, as much as any endeavor in life, has laws that explain the natural process and organization associated with the activity.

What is the first thing anyone does when playing a new game? He or she learns the rules, because without understanding the rules, there is no comprehension of how the game is played. A sale, just like a game, has rules, but unfortunately, these rules are not written on the inside of any box, and all too often, the rules to the game of sales are learned the hard way. To understand selling in a new market, a person must understand the laws that govern and rule the complexity of sales. The laws will provide insight into what can be expected, what will occur, and then what will happen next.

Science tells us that there are four immutable laws or forces that govern the universe: gravity, electromagnetism, strong nuclear force, and weak nuclear force. Similarly, there are four immutable laws or forces governing sales. These laws do not have to be obeyed from a legal sense; rather, the laws must be obeyed in order to succeed. Take gravity as an example. A man may leap off a tall building shrieking, "I don't believe in gravity." In this case, he doesn't break the law of gravity. It breaks him. There is no legal requirement to obey the law of gravity but if a person does not believe in gravity and jumps from a building, the law of gravity causes serious injury and, therefore, it triumphs. Failure to recognize these laws for what they are will result in disaster. Selling into a new market space, while not governed by the rules of sales, is in every sense attuned to the laws of sales. These laws of sales are as follows:

1. All things being equal, everyone will ultimately act in his or her self-interest.
2. Self-interest, properly understood, is a good thing.
3. People are generally risk-averse for gains and risk-seeking for losses.
4. What is not overtly positive is covertly negative.

These are the governing forces that we will consider in some detail. In addition, some laws, called secondary laws, are not universal (like the second law of thermodynamics), but they hold true *in their realm.*

These secondary laws are as follows:

- Nothing happens unless you make it happen.
- Divide and "concur."
- It is not the product.
- If you know what's going to happen, then you will know what to do.
- You know how to sell, but your prospect does not know how to purchase.
- Set the rules, and be prepared to change them.

Let's begin with the four laws of sales.

1. ALL THINGS BEING EQUAL, EVERYONE WILL ULTIMATELY ACT IN HIS OR HER SELF-INTEREST

This basic dictum of human nature is best evidenced in game theory, and more specifically, in the non-zero-sum game known as the Prisoner's Dilemma.

The Game

Two bad guys, referred to as Bonnie and Clyde, are caught near the scene of a crime. The police interrogate them separately. Each has to choose whether to confess and implicate the other. If both confess, they will each serve 10 years, half the maximum for cooperating with the prosecution. If neither confesses, they will each serve one year on a weapons charge. If one confesses, implicating the other, while the other remains silent, the first will go free, while the silent one will serve the maximum penalty of 20 years in prison.

The strategies in this case are simple: squeal or don't squeal. The payoffs (or penalties) are the prison sentences. This can be expressed simply in a typical game theory payoff table (Table 4.1).

The table reads thus: Each bad guy chooses one of the two strategies (Bonnie opts for one row in the figure, Clyde decides on a column to play). If Bonnie and Clyde both sing like canaries, they each get 10 years. If Bonnie rats Clyde out and Clyde remains silent, Bonnie goes free, while Clyde serves 20 years. If Bonnie doesn't squeal and Clyde does, Bonnie goes to prison for 20 years, while Clyde goes free. If neither confesses, they each serve one year (on the weapons charge).

Table 4.1 Game Theory Payoff

		Clyde	
		squeal	don't squeal
Bonnie	squeal	10, 10	0, 20
	don't squeal	20, 0	1, 1

What, then, are the rational strategies if both want to minimize the time they spend in prison? Bonnie might reason something like this: "Two things can happen: Clyde will either confess or he won't. If he confesses, and I don't, I get 20 years—10 years if I confess too—so in that case, it is best if I confess. On the other hand, if Clyde does not confess, and neither do I, I get a year; but in that case, if I confess I can go free. Either way, it's best if I confess. Therefore, I will confess."

However, Clyde will likely reason in the same way—both will therefore confess and go to prison for 10 years each. While if they had acted irrationally and kept quiet, they each could have gotten off with one year a piece.

What we learn from this narrative is that people, when they act rationally, do what is in their own best interest—a principle that is true for buyers as well as sellers. An extreme example of this principle manifests in the example of a sales manager who failed to recognize this law for what it is: He would call prospects toward the end of the quarter and explain that his employee bonus depended on closing that particular sale. His customers surely wondered why they should care and what is in it for them to buy his product.

Advanced sellers understand that their jobs would be easy if they only had to sell to companies. All they would have to do is demonstrate to the company that their product is the best fit for the need. However, salespeople do not sell to nonhuman entities called companies; rather, the sales are made to individuals who want to ensure that their best interests are served even while professing to have the good of the company at heart. Successful sellers also know that individuals may have interests that sometimes conflict, and it is the salespersons's job to ensure that all of the players feel that the needs of the individual and the company have been met when the final deal is stuck.

2. SELF INTEREST, PROPERLY UNDERSTOOD, IS A GOOD THING.

French Renaissance scholar Montaigne said long ago, "Even if I should not follow the straight road because of its straightness, I would follow it because I have found by experience that when all is said and done it is generally the happiest and most useful."[1] And the French political thinker Tocqueville noted, "In the United States there is hardly any talk of the beauty of virtue. However, they maintain that virtue is useful and prove it every day. American moralists do not pretend that one must sacrifice himself for his fellows because it is a fine thing to do so. . . . They therefore do not raise objections to men pursuing their interests, but they do all that they can to prove that it is in each man's interest to be good."[2] Finally, Roman rhetorician Marcus Fabius

Quintilian points out that "Providence has given this gift to man, that the honorable is the most profitable."

The lesson learned from all this is, in fact, the second of the laws of sales: Self-interest, properly understood, is a good thing. In other words, what is good for the individual is also good for the community at large. What makes this law tricky is that it applies to salespeople as much as it does to their prospects. What sets successful sellers apart is that they understand that acting in their prospects' best interests *is* in their greatest interest.

When skilled sellers approach a sale, they go in knowing that acting in the prospect's best interest means acting in the best interest of *all* of the individuals involved in making the buying decision. Although each person believes that he or she is doing what is right for the company, the truth is that the person is looking out for him- or herself first and the company's needs second.

Experienced sellers know this and use it as part of their sales strategy. A-players ask how each person in the process will benefit from closing the sale: *What's in it for them?* Asking this question, and being proactive about getting the answers, means that the seller will be able to present all communications in terms of how each person in the buying chain will benefit from the solution.

For example, knowing that a key person involved in making the buying decision is up for a promotion means that you can speak to how your product or service will serve that individual's future success. In that case, you are selling two things: career advancement and esteem from the person's bosses. It doesn't end there. When the up-and-comer's bosses are involved in the sale, the experienced sellers also ask themselves about the out-comes the bosses hope to gain from the purchase. Will choosing your product over a competitors' equal a "win" for the manager embroiled in an ongoing political rivalry? What of the rival? If that person is also involved in the buying decision, can you demonstrate that your product or service will show up in his or her "win" column as well. If someone else in the chain has another vendor at the top of his or her list, can you show that your solution will resolve the problems that keep him or her awake at night more effectively than the competitor's solution.

While learning about the company as a whole and selling to its best interest is vital to closing complex sales, learning to nav-igate the internal and interpersonal workings is just as important. Solid B-players make it their business to comb a prospect's Web site for information about its financials, customers, and market position. Exceptional B-players find out about the prospect's competitors.

3. PEOPLE ARE GENERALLY RISK-AVERSE FOR GAINS AND RISK-SEEKING FOR LOSSES

The third law of maverick selling is proven over and over again in examples such as the game show "Wheel of Fortune" and in countless gambling studies. The *escalation bias* also comes into play. In behavioral finance, escalation bias causes investors to invest more in money-losing investments. People are willing to compound losses for the sake of trying to "make it better" or prove they can "fix a wrong," all the while neglecting investment in successful ventures because there is no big win.

When we are winning, we are risk-averse; when we are losing, we are risk-seeking.

Buyers who are comfortable with the status quo are risk-averse. "Building the pain" is a basic principle of consultative selling that has roots in behavioral psychology. Getting someone to buy into an innovative or disruptive technology requires precisely that he or she is not comfortable with the status quo. Indeed, the person must feel like he or she is losing in order to overcome risk aversion. The new market seller intuitively understands that building the pain to a critical mass is crucial to making the sale.

4. WHAT IS NOT OVERTLY POSITIVE IS COVERTLY NEGATIVE

If you are not getting clear, positive feedback from a prospect, assume that something is wrong. No one likes to give or be on the receiving end of bad news. However, it is incumbent upon the salesperson to get to the bottom of any feedback that is not obviously positive, and that includes getting no feedback at all.

It is tempting to believe that a silent prospect is "just busy." It is comforting to believe that you are still being considered even when the prospect has stopped returning your calls or has started to miss commitments. In sales, deluding oneself into believing that tepid news or no news is good news is referred to as "happy ears," and that delusion leads to missed sales.

Here is the thing: We have had customers issue purchase orders for our products, all the while telling our competitors that they were still weighing their options. It isn't that the prospects are mean-spirited; rather, it is that the customer does not want to be the bearer of bad news.

> *Though it be honest, it is never good*
> *To bring bad news; give to a gracious message*
> *A host of tongues, but let ill tidings tell*
> *Themselves when they be felt.*[3]

The desire to avoid the uncomfortable position of being the one to tell the salesperson, "Sorry, we went with Vendor X," hearkens to the first law: Delivering bad news rarely serves the prospect's best interest.

Experienced sellers do not suffer from happy ears because they do not initiate the sale and then stand in the wings waiting to be chosen. Sellers need to elicit feedback from prospects throughout the buying process and enforce a cadence of communication that, if broken, signals that something is wrong. As they lead prospects from the initial sales call to signing a contract, A-players check to see how all of the people involved in the buying decision are feeling. Remember: At its most basic level, deciding to buy something is emotional. If this were not the case, consumers would always forgo the over-the-top SUV in favor of a fuel-efficient economy car that reliably transports them to work every day.

Such are the four immutable laws of sales. Let's look now at the secondary laws.

NOTHING HAPPENS UNLESS YOU MAKE IT HAPPEN

Newton's first law of motion, sometimes called the law of inertia, is often stated thusly: An object at rest tends to stay at rest and an object in motion tends to stay in motion with the same speed and in the same direction unless acted upon by an external force.[4] Companies at rest tend to stay that way unless acted upon by an external force. Lack of change is easy and comfortable. Unless there is some catalyst that propels an organization to buy something, it will not. Companies are moved to invest in high-dollar products and services when they perceive an imminent threat or there is an obvious and justifiable opportunity.

Skilled sellers know this and understand that what separates them from the pack is their ability to propel a company successfully to a closed sale even when external (or, often, internal) forces conspire to slow or stop the process. Whether companies are motivated by a threat (e.g., updating their computer systems in time for the new millennium) or an opportunity (e.g., enough capacity to handle an expected surge in demand for their products online), experienced sellers do not trust the company's natural work flow to end in a closed sale. The sellers need to lead and control the process. Leaving a sale up to the natural flow allows outside forces—like the prospect's undefined and poorly understood internal buying procedures—to slow or stop the process, thereby providing an opportunity for a competing salesperson to take the lead and the sale.

DIVIDE AND "CONCUR"

This is not a typo. The expected "conquer" is not actually in the lexicon, because a maverick sales person is always seeking the win-win solution. A sale is no place for conquest. However, it *is* a place for division, at least initially. The seller divides to gain cooperation or concurrence. He or she meets separately with each of the stakeholders in the client's decision chain, seeking buy-in from the oftentimes competing business, personal, and political interests of all the parties involved. The skilled sellers excel at getting everyone to agree that a single solution—the seller's solution—satisfies all of their best interests as well as the good of the company. Following is an example of an opportunity lost when a salesperson did not work the sale from all angles.

Frank and I meet for a quick beer after the end of the quarter, and I wanted to see how his new job was coming. Frank was at the bar when I arrived, and he did not look like the guy I had always known; he had forgone his beer in exchange for a martini. I pulled up a chair and asked how it was going. Frank explained that he lost a large deal to a smaller competitor and he was not sure why. I asked what he heard from his contact within the account. His champion, Ted, was shocked that his manager went with the smaller company. Ted had done the evaluation and had recommended Frank's product. Frank shared that he was so confident in what Ted was doing that he did not feel the need to meet with anyone else. Ted was so enthusiastic about the product and would give glowing feedback that it seemed like a waste of time talking to others within the organization. Ted had said that he was the sole decision maker and did not need anyone else's approval or buy-in. Ted felt that his manager did not understand the issues, even during the first presentation and demo, and did not ask any questions. I sat at the bar thinking to myself that if I was competing against Frank, I would go around Ted and meet with his manager one-on-one. Because I did not want to hurt Frank's feelings anymore then they had been, I keep my thoughts to myself.

Understanding each stakeholder's needs and desires cannot be accomplished in a group setting. Salespeople need to ensure that they spend as much one-on-one time as possible with each of the players in the decision chain. Incidentally, this is preferably face-to-face time; phone and/or e-mail do not work as well because reading a buyer's body language and expressions is important for getting to the heart of his or her concerns. The seller's goal is to leave each person in the buying chain feeling confident that the seller is on his or her side; this leads to the win-win where everyone concurs.

The skilled seller is rarely involved in a bake-off without having met previously with all or most of the participants. Earning buyers' confidence—and salespeople need to earn it—does not happen in a group meeting and can never happen in a group situation where multiple vendors will be presenting their solutions. In a group setting, buyers present a united front of poker faces. The standard response to any seller's request for feedback in that setting will be, "We'll get back to you on that."

Ideally, the first "official" meeting will not be a group meeting in which you have to deliver a blanket sales pitch to multiple decision makers with multiple agendas. In the best situation, you will be able to meet individually with key players without even the suggestion that there will be a large group meeting. However, if you cannot avoid a group meeting, do what successful sellers need to do: Request a short, informal tête-à-tête with each of the key decision makers ahead of the group session. This will give you an opportunity to get each person's unguarded point of view and learn how you can best address that person's concerns. Gathering this information prior to a group meeting gives you an opportunity to tailor your presentation to the individual agendas in the meeting. You will not have to worry about the united front, and you will set yourself apart from B-players who will go in hoping that their stock presentation will work for all stakeholders.

IT IS NOT THE PRODUCT

The Bloomberg Terminal has 27,000 features that have all the bells and whistles, and yet not one of them differentiates itself from the rest. Not one. It is no longer enough to sell products; your product or service—which still needs to be great—is merely the ticket to the dance. It gets you in, but the modern buyer is not buying a product; he or she is buying solutions to his or her problem and business outcomes. Top sellers understand the competitive landscapes in which their prospects operate, and they know about innovations and standard practices in their targets' industries. These top sellers know their prospects' customers. Before the first sales call, the seller needs to have scoured prospects' Web sites and other industry sources to get a firm grasp of the company's financials, reputation, market position, and prospects for the future. Successful sellers do all of this because they know that products are not at the top of customers' lists of business concerns. Results are what drives companies and are the focus.

If you are relying on your product and not on your skill as a professional salesperson, then you are breaking this law. We often hear salespeople state that if only their product had this feature or that feature, then they could sell. My comment to this is, "So what? If you are dependent on the product to sell itself, the company would not need salespeople."

Seasoned salespeople routinely close sales using products that are not market leaders—or even well known. They beat the competition by selling results that are best suited to their customers' immediate needs, and that anticipate their future needs. A-players keep their customers engaged in the sales process and confident that they made the best decisions for themselves and their companies. The law of "It is not the product" puts the responsibility of selling where it needs to be: on the salesperson. Until you acknowledge that responsibility and take ownership of the sale, you will not reach your potential.

IF YOU KNOW WHAT'S GOING TO HAPPEN, THEN YOU KNOW WHAT TO DO

This law is about applying your experience and ability to interrupt signals that the prospect is sending by taking corrective action before it is too late. The ability to anticipate what can go wrong and find a way to prevent it is the essence of this law.

In hindsight, everything is crystal clear: the unreturned phone calls, the slipped deadlines, and the prospect's less-than-enthusiastic response to a demonstration. In hindsight, when a deal falls through, the constant refrain from a seller is, "I knew that that was going to happen."

> Kevin and I had lunch, and he shared with me that his milliondollar deal had gone to our competitor. I asked what happened, and he said that they really liked our solution but kept asking us about our support for the ISO standard. Ken felt that he had

responded appropriately and explained that we would have ISO support within the year. Ken shared that he had a sinking feeling that the deal was not going his way and stated that "he knew that this was going to happen." I was shocked and asked, "If you knew it was going south, why did you not do something to stop it?" Kevin shared that he was just hoping that the issue would go away because it was a small issue that had no real business impact. I dug deeper and asked how long ago the client showed interest in this standard, and Kevin said that it was just after his competitor made their presentation. At that time, several people within the account brought up the idea of needing ISO support.

Sellers need to pay attention to the process and regularly ask themselves, "What's going to happen next?" and "What can go wrong?" Sometimes the answers are clear; the sales process is progressing the way that most of your successes have, and you know that it is smooth sailing until you close the sale. On the other hand, when the sale is not going exactly as planned, asking the aforementioned questions offers sellers the opportunity to resolve issues before these problems unleash a deal-killing blow. A-players get the answers to these questions by calling on past experiences, checking in with the prospect, and looking for previously unnoticed signs of trouble.

Salespeople need to listen to that internal voice that says, "Hey, I think something is wrong, and I think I need to do something about this problem." A strong action needs to be taken. Waiting till that voice is proven correct is breaking this law. In your heart, you know that you are missing something and that either your competitor is cutting you off at your knees or there is a person within the account that you have misread.

YOU KNOW HOW TO SELL, BUT YOUR PROSPECT DOES NOT KNOW HOW TO PURCHASE

Although end users will insist that it only takes a few days to get a purchase order approved and signed at their companies, experienced sellers know this is not true. Very few people in an organization have extensive experience making major purchases in their companies, least of all business and technical users. While their intentions are good, the fact is that there are very few occasions when a very large expenditure does not need multiple levels of approval. Complex buying goes through multiple levels of approval and review before a company proceeds. This is where A-players excel.

Jerry was frustrated with his new opportunity because the deal seemed stalled and after several meetings with his champion, his promises of progress had all turned into nothing but more "next steps." During coffee, I asked Jerry what was his champion's role with the account. Jerry shared that he was a very promising manager who is new to the group but really wants to make an impact. I asked who else is behind the purchase of the product. Jerry explained that the champion's whole team was on board. I quickly asked who outside the champion's team had bought into the vision of what the product could do for their organization. Jerry shared that the champion wanted to manage that and did not want vendors contacting anyone outside his team. I asked if the champion had purchased anything from anyone else before, as evidence that he would know the process. Jerry said that he had asked and that he had not. Hum, I thought to myself. I remembered buying my first house and all the issues that surrounded it, from mortgages to inspections and closing costs. If it was not for my trusted real estate agent, I would have made several very expensive mistakes. My agent led me through the process after understanding what I was looking for and could afford. The realtor explained what I should expect and what to prepare for during the transaction. Before going through the home buying process, I really had no appreciation for what real estate agents do and the value they provided, and I learned that I did not know how to purchase real estate.

The end user has a job in the company, and buying is not his or her primary function. In fact, it is unlikely that buying anything other than routine office supplies is the job for any one person. That said, it is the seller's job to learn the process and be the shepherd for those making the buying decisions. This is the seller's job because part of making the sale is making the buying process easy. Once a prospect realizes that it takes more than a few days to get a purchase order approved, the process will stall. That is, the process will stall until a seller comes in and teaches the buyer how his or her company makes major purchases.

SET THE RULES, AND BE PREPARED TO CHANGE THEM

In the best-case scenario, you are the first vendor that a prospect meets, which means that you can establish the rules. The rules present the criteria that the buyer should be looking for to make a sound purchasing decision. Remember, the buyer does not know how to buy a solution to his or her business problem. The new market seller needs to use those rules to make the case that his or her solution is the best one to meet the prospect's needs. While the seller is establishing the rules, he or she is also setting traps for sales competitors. The new market seller's rules not only position his or her product as the best solution for the customer; he or she also positions the competitor's products as poor options. It is not that competing solutions are inherently bad; rather, it is that those solutions do not meet the criteria set forth in the new market seller's rules. Therefore, the competing product will not satisfy the customer's needs.

For example, a seller will tell the customer that the best solution to his or her business problem is one that conforms to established industry standards. Such a solution would be compatible with technologies that the customer already uses and positions the company for smoother upgrades, future growth, and compatibility with soon-to-be released peripheral products. Because the standard is so widely accepted, the buyer will have many options for training, support, and service. The rule, then, is that the customer should only consider using a standards-based solution, one of which the successful seller happens to be selling.

The rule also functions as a trap. The competitor has a workable solution, too. However, the competing product uses a proprietary technology. When the competition comes calling, and touting his product's innovativeness, the customer will already be of the mind that a proprietary solution limits his or her options for upgrades, growth, compatibility, and support.

On the other hand, even the most aggressive seller cannot be the first vendor to talk to a prospect every time. In that case, the seller does two things. First, he or she determines the traps and rules set by the competition, and then the seller prepares well-crafted responses in his counter-presentation.

Justin was competing for a new opportunity within the largest account inside his territory, and unfortunately, his competitor was the industry leader with the largest market share. I know Justin is a talented and experienced salesperson who had competed for large deals before and won most, but in this instance, the odds were certainly against him. When I had lunch with Justin to compare notes on each other's progress within our respective territories, he showed no sign of weakness about this opportunity but rather had a secret weapon that he felt confident would turn the tide his way. I asked about it, looking for any new information I could find. Justin shared that his large account was favoring a more stable and established vendor, but he had a feeling that responsiveness was also a characteristic that was highly valued. Justin explained that he made this the one and most important characteristic. He scheduled reference visits to other customers with whom he had worked successfully and had them explain how Justin had gotten the company to do backflips to meet new requirements and to have the product work with their unique situation. Justin provided good references on how he would be flexible and responsive to this company. In other words, he showed them just how important they would be to him and his company. Justin constantly built doubt about his competitor's ability to respond to unique needs and the clients need for on-site support with experienced consultants. I now understood why Justin is so successful.

To accomplish those two things, the seller does a side-by-side comparison of his or her product's benefits versus the competitors' offerings. You can learn about a competing product's benefits and features by studying the company Web site. A side-by-side comparison gives the seller insight into how the competitor would have positioned the seller's product. The A-player takes the opportunity to reposition the competitor's strengths as weaknesses that the prospect should avoid at all costs. Following are a few traps and rules:

- *Standards.* If the competing product does not conform to industry standards, the skilled seller will position that product as one that buyers will have trouble using outside of their own companies. If the product does not conform to standards, their partners and customers will be shut out. On the other hand, if the seller's product does not conform to an established standard, the seller may be able to prove that the existing standard is changing and that buyers will have a head start while their competitors are playing catch-up.
- *Features.* Demonstrate how their product features serve their prospects' needs, while a competing product's features may not be as effective.
- *Integration with other products.* If a competing product does not integrate with buyers' existing product investments, it can be positioned as cost-prohibitive, forcing buyers to replace their existing products as well.
- *Financial stability.* Being able to tout your company's financial position will cause prospects to examine your competitors' financial positions more closely. The last thing that they want is to be stuck trying to find support for a product developed by a company that has gone out of business.
- *Local support.* If your product can be supported locally versus a competitor's product that may require shipping or waiting to have a technician flown in, your product will be a lot more attractive to prospects. Companies want to know that they will suffer a minimum amount of lost productivity should the product need servicing or if end users need technical support.

- *Market share.* Like financial stability, higher or increasing market share tells customers that your company will be around in the future.
- *Future product releases.* Customers want to know that your company is keeping up with advances in the marketplace. If your company has an aggressive release schedule, it will give them comfort that you will be able to keep up. On the other hand, a competitor's aggressive release schedule might be positioned as a negative; rapid deployments might indicate inadequate testing. An additional position would be that an aggressive release might require frequent expensive upgrades.

If you cannot establish the rules or change those that your competitors have set, you can encourage prospects to look at your weakest competitor. It is unlikely that the weaker competitor will win the business, but introducing another player could buy you extra time to strengthen your position.

Think about each of these laws and how they have worked in your sales. We will be referencing these laws in the following chapter, and you will see how they work in conjunction with the maverick method and increase your level of success.

Chapter 5

The Selling-in-a-New-Market Skill Set

Since our focus for this book is on the business-to-business complex sale, and you, our target reader, is someone who has several years of sales experience, we will not review the basic selling skills but rather focus on the skills that have separated mavericks from the rest of the crowd.

The interpersonal sale is what we refer to as the simple sale. Advanced selling skills are needed with the complex sale, because, with the complex sale, you are selling to a group of people but selling to them in very different ways. That said, the interpersonal skills of building rapport, questioning, building interest, and closing are extremely vital for success in business-to-business selling.

DEFINING THE COMPLEX SALE

It is important to define the type of sale that we are covering in this book. The complex sale has several characteristics. First, it involves selling to an organization, meaning that there will be several people and several groups playing some role in the purchasing decision. Second, the product is complex in many ways, such as the features and functions that can be beyond the knowledge of a single person. The natural side effects of the complexities are that the complex sale takes a considerable amount of time, the cost of the product is high, and there are several competing alternatives to solve the problem.

With this understanding of the complex sale, it becomes clear that marketing will have limited ability to do anything more than create awareness. The complexity will also limit what the product can do on its own—unlike a simple sale, where the marketing and product are dominant and the sales function can be completed with classic selling techniques.

The complex sale requires an additional skill set, and we will describe what those skills are and how they are to be applied and perfected. Think back to the deals that you have lost in your past: What did each have in common? Most likely they were deals where you were not sure what to do next, deals that had lost momentum, and deals that you certainly did not have control over. Now, think of the deals that you have won over the years. These were deals where you knew exactly what to do next; they had momentum, and you were in control.

Now that we have outlined and described previously the characteristics that make up and are necessary to excel in sales, we will build on those characteristics to the next level: skills. Since we are addressing the very best and most successful of salespeople, we are assuming that you have a strong understanding of the basic interpersonal selling skills like prospecting, qualifying, questioning, building interest, and closing. There are hundreds of books on interpersonal sales topics, and we feel there is no need to present them here. We would like to focus on the skills that take people from the A-player level and make them mavericks. The skills that we will describe are all, again, targeted to the complex sale, and we will describe why the skills of the complex sale are different than those of the interpersonal sale. These skills are not hard to learn or to develop, but a surprising few are even aware of them.

"THERE ARE SEVERAL MEETINGS AND EVALUATIONS AND THEN SOMETHING MAGICAL HAPPENS"

I remember being in an interview with the founder and CEO of a well-funded start-up, and I was interested in understanding their sales process. Even though they did not have a product in the marketplace for long, they had closed deals with several large customers. The CEO had been one of the key players in each of the deals, presenting his company's direction and explaining the commitment that they had for their first customers. With the CEO so involved in the sales process and in some cases being the leader of a particular deal, I felt that he would have a great deal of insight into how best to drive the process. When I posed the question, "What is your sales process?" he responded very cavalierly, stating that there would be a series of meetings, presentations, and an evaluation phase. I then pressed and said, "OK, but how do you go from that evaluation phase to getting them to purchase?" And he got a little out of sorts and responded, "Well, something magical happens."

I suspected that he may not have known the answer, but I did not want to offend him, so I asked about the last deal in which he was directly involved in the closing. He explained that it was the last week of the quarter, and it was the only deal that was possible. He had flown in the night before and was aggressively pushing the CEO of the prospective customer for a purchase order. The CEO and his team spent the evening polishing their pitch and thinking over the objections. The CEO explained that the meeting went well, so I asked what the "magical" item was that made the deal happen. The CEO sheepishly explained that he offered a large discount and several days of free consulting. So that was the magical thing that happened? Yes, the CEO said. *Well*, I thought to myself, *that is some process.* I'm sure that the CEO does not empower the sales force to generously discount and give away free services without executive review and approval.

You will learn that you do not need any magic tricks to close complex deals in a timely and predictable manner. What this CEO and, frankly, 97 percent of the salespeople I know do not understand is that there is a decision path that organizations take when they purchase. That decision path can be short-cut with discounts, and you can roll the dice on the last day of the quarter; but if you know the path and develop the skills to control it, you can win the deal in a repeatable and predictable manner.

The complex sale is more than just a string of simple sales, and it is very dangerous to think of the complex sale as just a series of selling individuals, because if you sell each individual without understanding his or her unique needs and vantage points, you will end up confusing instead of convincing. The complex sale involves several people, all of whom who have their own agenda and their own view of what is good for the company and, more importantly, what is good for them. The complex sale deserves its name because there is no single decision maker; there are people who can veto a decision, but there needs to be consensus at some minimum level. Several of the characteristics of the complex sale make it difficult to build this consensus, including the time gaps between meetings and the lack of interest that curtain stakeholders will have for dealing with salespeople.

Figure 5.1 The skills of the complex sale.

The skills needed to complete the complex sale are not taught by any sales training classes and are not addressed in any book. The necessary skills fall into three key areas: direction, momentum, and control, as shown in Figure 5.1.

DIRECTION

Of course, everyone knows that you want to go straight to getting a purchase order, right? Yes, but how exactly does one get there? That is the hard part. The CEO in the previous example knew that there were presentations and a couple demos and even a lengthy evaluation process, but he did not know how to connect all that activity to getting the order. From his perspective, it was that magical meeting that was driven by his desperation to make a quarterly goal and to keep the board of directors from replacing him. The magical event was him buying the business with a low-ball bid and supplementing it with free services. This is the norm and not the exception. The exception is knowing the process and the people involved in the process and mapping that out so that you know where you are and where you are going.

As in the physical world, when you want to go from point A to point B, you get a map that shows the routes and sometimes the terrain. How one actual gets from point A to B is up to the individual. The problem in the world of the complex sale is that since so few have been successful in navigating the terrain and routes, these paths are mostly in people's heads and are not expressed on paper. It is true that most salespeople can list how they go from prospect to closure, but for anyone who has not been consistently successful in the complex sales, that list does not take into account enough detail or contingency to show someone else how to navigate it. As author H. Stanley Judd says, "A good plan is like a road map: it shows the final destination and usually the best way to get there."

The map to money, as we will refer to it in this book, and as we will cover in more detail in Chapter 6, is how the maverick navigates the opportunities. The map to money is the big picture and the game board of the complex sale. There is good reason why no other sales book describes the map; it is because no one really writes it down. The salespeople that I have studied have it in their heads and have built their strategies on top of it, but they do not take the time to document it.

Our clients often say we have tried the blue sheets or sales process models before, and no one uses them. It is true there are several interpretations of documenting the sales process, including war books, win plans, flight plans, and plan letters. We have never seen any organization really be successful from using any of them, although sales management has always been supportive of them. The reason these documents have failed over and over again is that they are not an accurate representation of the terrain of the complex sale. They are a sequential list of actions and people, but they miss the key milestones, overlook what your competitors are doing, and fail to anticipate what can go wrong. At the individual level, these documents lack the unique style and strategy that each salesperson will employ. Without the individual salesperson buying into the process, the document just becomes an administrative artifact or check-box item, and no real value is gained. These documents also do not take into account the unique characteristics of selling a particular product to a particular account.

The map to money is meant to cover the major components of the selling effort and is intended to be unique to both the product and the individual seller.

In the culinary world, the map is a recipe. A recipe is a list of ingredients and instructions to prepare a dish. A recipe makes the assumption that you have the basic skills and cooking utensils. According to Thomas Keller, chef and owner of The French Laundry, "A cookbook must have recipes, but it shouldn't be a blueprint. It should be more inspirational; it should be a guide." The map to money has some of the same characteristics as a recipe in that there are general recipes that cover how to sell a particular product and make the assumption that the reader has basic selling skills and has access to selling tools. The recipe analogy is also applicable because skilled chefs will vary the recipe to their own abilities and tastes. The excellent chefs have also prepared dishes many times without referring to a written recipe; instead, they go from a instinctive state to create something that is unique to them.

Jerry was the most successful salesperson I had ever met at the time, and he was nice enough to spend time with me and help me understand what made a great salesperson. I would quiz him for hours about his deals and pull out of him what made him so successful. After dinner one night, he shared that what other salespeople do not understand is that organizations have two separate yet equally important parts of the deal: the technical decision, meaning which product fits the functional requirements best, and the business decision, meaning which product fits the overall economics of the company. He said that most salespeople become good at one or the other, but almost no one becomes good at both. Jerry said he figured this out early in his career and became good at both.

MOMENTUM

The momentum of a complex sale can be driven by the prospect, which is fine if it is moving at the pace that you are happy with, but it never is. Since the prospect is not trained in how to purchase your product, it is up to the salesperson to set and maintain the momentum of the deal. This skill is as rare as the understanding of the process, and even more so is someone who can actual maintain the momentum without rushing the prospect or killing the deal.

So, how do you build momentum?

Momentum is built by giving each player a strong personal reason to take action and to be part of that action. Applying the "divide and concur" natural law of sales from Chapter 4 will give you the opportunity to not depend on any one player but rather to build interest and gain insights from many different perspectives.

> Dave had great momentum-maintaining skills, for he rarely ate a meal alone. Dave would find a good breakfast place close to each of his target accounts and would invite key players to breakfast, and the busier people liked breakfast because it did not interfere with their schedule and it was a nice way to get to know each other. Dave would never invite more than one person to breakfast,

and he would match the restaurant to the individual he was inviting. Dave enjoyed the social aspect of meeting people off-site and would often wait for the prospect to bring up business so as to not make people feel pressured or obligated to talk about it. Dave was able to build lasting relationships because he was focused on the personal wins that each person was looking for, and, in return, people would be great references for him. Dave knew that treating people to a meal was not in any way a new idea, but what was unique is that Dave did not just do it when he wanted information; he did it even when he did not have an agenda.

Once you have met the players, the simplest and yet most powerful way to build momentum is to create a reason for the next communication and settle on a time and date to communicate. This simple method will keep the ball rolling, and even if the next communication is a 10-minute phone call, it keeps the line of communication open and active.

Begin with the end in mind. The prospect is purchasing a product to gain some business benefit; they want that benefit by some date, and it is that end date that will then drive every decision. So, momentum must be built with that deadline in mind, and the action plan must be based on it. Once that deadline has been agreed upon, you now have the reason why every step must be completed by its own deadline and why each person in the process needs to communicate with you and keep the deal moving.

When you have momentum, you sense it and it feels good. You are not pushing nor pulling; you are simply working together on a joint objective.

If you lose momentum, it is a very important sign that something is wrong, and your attention is needed immediately.

CONTROL

"Let's see what they have to say." This is what we hear most B-players say before a sales call. The B-players and even most A-players have no real control over the deal; they are simply responding to the prospect and asking what they would like to do next. What a maverick does differently is to focus the prospect on what he or she wants to do next and leads the prospect through the buying process. Control is built from two attributes: being a leader and being proactive. As author Vance Packard said, "Leadership appears to be the art of getting others to want to do something you are convinced should be done."

Leadership is a big part of controlling the deal, because once you know where you are going, you need to lead your prospect through the process. Of course, they need to be willing to be led, which means you need to have added enough value to gain their trust. As the deal leader, it is your responsibility to elicit each player's concerns and to answer his or her questions. Leadership is not relying on anyone else other than you to capture the deal. Leadership is not just moving the prospect from one step to the next, but leading the prospect to what the decision criteria are and the rules that criteria are based on.

Being proactive is knowing what to do next and taking the actions to accomplish it. It is preventing what you know can go wrong and playing the game at least one move ahead.

Once you know where you are going, you need to know how you are going to get there and have enough momentum to arrive by the deadline you have set. How do you control the deal? The hardest and most advanced skill is controlling the sale.

No one likes to be controlled, and, especially when you are pay-ing money, the last thing you want is someone telling you what to do. Yet when we are in unfamiliar waters, we want someone to guide or even to lead us. So it is a key differentiator of the maverick seller that he or she knows how to control the selling process without offending or alienating buyers or making them feel controlled.

The direction that the map to money will give you and the momentum that we have created will require the leadership to control the deal.

Applying the natural laws of sales will give us the rules by which the game is played. The law that most apply to control-ling the deal is this: You may know how to sell, but your prospect does not know how to buy. Once you internalize this law, you understand that it is the salespeople's responsibility to lead the sale; whether they take that responsibility or not, it is theirs. If you know what is going to happen, then you know what to do. By anticipating what is going to happen, both right and wrong, you are prepared to act and not just to react. By building these laws into your map, your thinking, and your strat-egy, it will become natural to understand why things happen the way they do and how you can control them.

How do you know if you are in control of the deal? You will know when you are in control by the way your prospects react to your requests. They will be asking for your help and support to justify their decision, and they will be cooperative and con-firming of your suggestions. Testing for control should be done with every communication by simply requesting an item of information or action and seeing if the prospect complies.

Quid pro quo is the most powerful technique to control a deal. Once a prospect shows interest in your product, he or she will naturally request something from you, and this is where most salespeople miss the point. The natural response a salesperson has to a prospect's request is to immediately support the request with what he or she can give, which is the worst thing you can do because this is the opportunity to get what you want, when you want it.

ROGUE WAVE CASE STUDY

Rogue Wave Software ran into a growth challenge in 1998 when I began working there. I noticed that the product pricing was on the Web site, which meant prospects did not need to call to get pricing, and since they did not call, there was no dialogue. The result of the removal was that the number of inbound calls more than doubled. My role was a regional manager in what was the lowest-performing region at the time. I wanted to first learn how things were being done, to see what could be done to increase revenue. I spent a week listening in on calls that the inside team would make, and I noticed that anytime someone would ask for something, the salesperson would jump to get it, which is great service but poor selling. When a prospect asks for something, it is a good time to ask for something in return; in fact, it is the perfect time to ask for something in return. The sales team expanded their use of quid pro quo to exchange evaluation copies for meetings, discounts for introduction to senior management, and technical support for a deeper understand of what they wanted to accomplish. The inside sales leaders were so impressed with what they were able to get with this selling skill that they coined the term

---

"push-back selling," and with this single skill, the team was able to dramatically increase the amount of control they had over each deal. Within two years, we were able to build the largest and fastest-growing region in the company. So, quid pro quo needs to be built into each interaction with the prospect, and the amount of preparation needs to be established so that you are matching their requests with getting the things you need. We have all experienced asking for something that we need, and if we do not have something to exchange, we are at the mercy of the prospect. We also know that prospects will not be shy in demanding whatever they want to achieve their own objective.

Following are some tips on how to increase your control:

1. Determine what the prospect will be requesting at each milestone, and be prepared to request one of three things in exchange for their request. A pattern will appear as to what the prospect will request at each of the touch points of the sales process, and it is important to know what he or she will be asking for and what you will need, so that a fair and friendly exchange can take place. The smart thing to do is to ask for the largest and most viable item without over-reaching, so that the progress of the transaction can move forward.

2. The maverick never gives the prospect anything without requesting something in return. As salespeople, we feel obligated to give prospects anything that they ask for, but in reality we are really giving away our control of the process.

3. In the map to money, you will have natural points where a request will arise and you will require a prepared list of things that you will need to advance the deal.

Of course, there are many important skills needed to create and win in a new market, but without momentum, direction, and control, your chances of winning are greatly diminished. It is hard to imagine any deal where you are going in the right direction, have consistent momentum, and are controlling the decision criteria, but somehow lose. With these new selling skills, winning will become the natural outcome, and you will be able build a repeatable process to close each deal.

Chapter 6

Creating the Sales Process Map for Selling in a New Market

The new product in the new market requires thinking through the sales process completely and understanding how each milestone is different than other products that have been sold. At the highest levels, the milestones are the same as in an existing market but how each milestone is achieved and transitioned is much more complex.

The sales process map—which we call the map to money because that is the ultimate goal—is one of the simplest and least understood facets of the complex selling process. Indeed, it is generally the missing link in the sales process. Some sales strategies discuss the players and their buying roles or perhaps have a list of milestones that need to be achieved, but we've not yet come across anyone who develops a real map—a treasure map, if you will—that describes the exact number of steps between milestones and markers and landmarks and that guides you to "X," the treasure. A good treasure map will tell you which swamps have man-eating alligators and which just have annoying mosquitoes; it will tell you where there is quicksand and perhaps even what to do if you get stuck in it; and it will point out any other potential traps and dangers. So will our map to money.

We have stated that A-players will be able to label the general things that need to be done to get a purchase order, but they will usually question prospects about what they'd like to do next instead of leading them through the map to money. Without the map to money, salespeople are on what amounts to a wild goose chase: They may occasionally catch a goose, but it is almost purely a matter of luck. Perhaps a better analogy would be a treasure hunt like that in the movie *National Treasure*: The hero has to unravel a set of mysteries, moving from one difficult clue to the next, as he seeks the treasure. At each step, our hero must be able to interpret correctly enigmatic poems (or signals) to determine his next move. Even our maverick would find it challenging. The problem, of course, with hunting treasure without a good map is that it is reactionary; a salesperson without a good map has no control over the process and is prone to error when interpreting clues.

We've seen sales models that suggest the salesperson make a list of all the steps in the sales process and share it with the prospect. One trouble with this approach is that, while many prospects are willing to help and even guide, they are rarely inclined to do the salesperson's job. Each has his prescribed role; lines should be respected and not crossed. We've actually tried sharing a list of the sales steps with prospects ourselves, only to watch the prospect roll his or her eyes and ignore the list. The main problem, of course, is that these lists tend to be linear; they go in sequence and are single-threaded and usually assume that one person can accomplish each item on the list.

That said, these lists can be a good starting point for developing a process map. Each item on the list needs to be matched to the correct player, and items that can be done concurrently (versus sequentially) need to be identified. The map provides a step-by-step visual representation of what needs to happen and what might go wrong, so that the seller can be ready with a response for all contingencies. It turns the treasure hunt into a treasure map, preparing the seller with the skills he or she will need, when he or she needs them, to be proactive in the sales process.

Incidentally, the map to money complements the law that states, "You know how to sell, but your prospect does not know how to purchase." The map provides the seller with a how-to guide from the buyer's perspective.

The main reason that sellers do not have a map in their minds, or as part of their strategy, is that maps take a great deal of thought and reflection. Complex deals sometimes take more than a year to complete. It is just natural—because it is easier—to take an action and then respond to the prospect's response to your action rather than try to envision the map, see the whole picture, and lead each player in the prospect company to closure.

"SO WHAT HAPPENED?"

What happens all too often is that an introductory call is made to a kingpin account, and the sales rep brings in the rock star presenter. Almost every organization has the person who can share the vision better than anyone else; he or she most likely built the slide deck that all others use as the corporate standard. So the rock star presenter comes in all hyped up on coffee and goodwill. He builds the vision piece by piece, and the buyers connect with him, and he talks fast and loose with the facts and the state of the product.

More often than not, the amount of time that was allocated for the meeting is expired but there are still 15 slides to go. The audience is still enthralled, but stomachs begin to grumble, and another group needs the meeting room, and other priorities of everyday work life begin to rear their ugly heads. The prospect apologizes, and the projector is taken to its next appointment. The sales team is ushered to the lobby, and it is all smiles and handshakes with the proverbial "let's talk soon" goodbye. The rock star from corporate is all too pleased with yet another standing ovation.

The salesperson makes a determination of forecast-ability based on something that is simply not understood. In this case, Mr. Rock Star returns to corporate with stories of the brilliant conquest and assures the executive team that a huge win is imminent; it is all but closed. Of course, the salesperson follows up, offering a proposal and a contract for the prospect's lawyer to review and is met with a wall of silence. He gets the brush-off. Corporate wants to know what happened and wrongly concludes that the salesperson somehow screwed up a slam-dunk deal. The salesperson is accused of incompetence and is let go.

Now you may be saying to yourself that it's so obvious: They didn't close for the next meeting, or they somehow misread what the prospect wanted or needed. Both are right. But these problems are endemic and do not affect just the rookie but the 20-year veteran as well. Generally, it is the difference between the B-player and the maverick. The B-player is reacting to the whims of the prospect rather than leading the prospect through a process to a business decision.

The map to money is necessary because it is simply too much to ask for a salesperson to master all of the selling skills, integrate them into his or her personality, and then apply them in the field. The only logical solution is to break down the process into its component parts—understandable parts that can be learned and practiced so that, once in the field, the salesperson can know what to do and how to do it.

You will find that each product and salesperson will have a unique map to money, with very different characteristics and skills that will be needed to move the process forward to the goal. Mavericks may not draw it or have an artifact that they call a map, but it is in their head and wired into their DNA. Without this map, salespeople are hunting and pecking, trying to find their way to closing a deal.

The biggest blank spot on most maps to money is between the first call and the business sale (terms we shall define in a moment). So often, the salesperson does not even understand what mechanically happens in this process, never mind having any control or leadership through the process. The B-player generally has a pretty good handle on the first call—the first landmark on the map—and on the back-end process of dealing with purchasing. But he generally falls apart in the middle: controlling the process of the decision and the allocation of the budget.

Let's look now at the key facets of every sales call:

- What is the objective of the call?
- What are they going to ask for? What are three things that I will ask for in return?
- How will I know if we can move forward? What is the next forward movement?
- What has our competitor been doing?
- What is the next touch point that we can get agreement on?

100

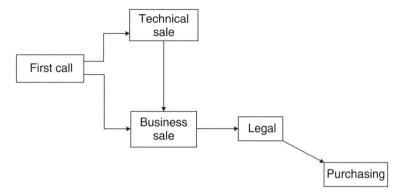

Figure 6.1 The map to money.

Figure 6.1 is a very general outline of the sales process or map to money. Note that the first two arrows on the left are not straight lines but rather are a bit convoluted. So is the process. And remember, this is the blank spot and the most difficult terrain on most maps to money. The following sections define each stage of this map.

FIRST CALL

The first call is typically a meeting arranged through effective prospecting that has won a salesperson a seat at the table. The objective of the first call is to find out if there is a match between what your product does and the prospect's pain. The next step is to determine who the stakeholders are and to turn the person with whom you are meeting into an ally: a guide at worst and an advocate at best. The advocate not only tells you what's going on but takes you to the economic buyer, which is the desired outcome of the first call: an introduction to the economic or business buyer, the person who controls the purse strings.

MEET WITH EACH STAKEHOLDER
INDIVIDUALLY

In that wasteland between the first call and the business sale lies, among other potential traps, meetings with each of the stakeholders individually. The purpose of these meetings is to find out what each person needs—be it financial, political, or economic—and work out how you can meet those needs.

TECHNICAL SALE

Salespeople tend to be optimistic. Imagine a 15-year-old going into a Porsche dealership. He knows everything there is to know about Porsches. He knows just what he wants: year, make, model, color, and interior, even custom stereo system. The salesperson is all excited (of course, unaware of the child's age) and begins to draw up the paperwork. Just then the boy's father comes in and, a bit perturbed, says, "Son, we're already late for practice—get in the car."

The technical sale is the winning over of the end user of your product or service. The technical buyer, like the 15-year-old Porsche shopper, does not have decision-making authority. He cannot write the check. The technical buyer must take you to the economic—or business—buyer.

The technical sale evolves in stages. These stages are natural, and by knowing and understanding them, you can control prospects as they progress through them. The stages of the gaining the technical sale are as follows:

- Establish that there is something that needs to be solved.
- Become a possible solution.
- Become the preferred solution.
- Lock out the alternative solutions.

BUSINESS SALE

The business sale is completed when there is an irreversible legal commitment, typically a purchase order or signed contract. The business buyer, in contrast with the technical buyer, can write the check. Of course, he or she is likely to take you to the technical buyer to see if your product actually works. The business buyer has political, financial, or user experience, but not usually technical experience.

Too often, the business sale is not begun until the technical sale is completed. This is far too late and leads to false deals and deals that take longer and become smaller. The technical sale is largely worthless without the business sale. The business sale should begin at the same time, and the selling should continue concurrently.

The business sale is harder because the business players do not know why they are dealing with you—because they haven't made a decision to select you yet. Quid pro quo should be used as the method to be introduced to the person who will sponsor you from a financial standpoint. A relationship will need to be established with each of the people who will need to approve the purchase, and in each case, they will need to know why they are approving this option in comparison to all the other alternative solutions to their problem. The key mistake is not working this angle from the beginning and not learning the language of the businesspeople. Businesspeople focus on the operations and leadership issues; they care about revenue, expense, and the competitiveness of the business and want to know how this purchase will affect these areas of the business. They do not care about the bells and whistles of the product. They do not want to see demos, but they do want to learn about your company's suitability as a business partner. And they care about testimonials from other companies that have used your product.

Use the business sale to jointly develop a business justification, which is both needed to prove that the purchase makes business sense and a powerful tool to keep the momentum going.

LEGAL

The legal aspect of a sale is a technicality; the bulk of the hard work has been done. This is a matter of crossing the *t*'s and dotting the *i*'s and agreeing on a legal contract that can be passed on to purchasing.

PURCHASING

There may be some negotiation of terms left to do, but if you have sold properly, the negotiations should go largely in your favor. In the sale of an innovation or disruptive technology, there are, by definition, no competitors. The product is quite literally unique in the marketplace. But there is always competition with other uses of money or with internal solutions.

SALES CARTOGRAPHY

Making maps to money seems to be an art lost with the pirates of yore. Sales map making is a skill rarely if ever taught; many models treat the organization as a single person rather than as a group of disparate individuals with different needs and different desires. These other models also tend to focus on reacting to a prospect's requests rather than leading the prospect step-by-step to the purchase.

The maverick establishes a map to money early and quickly and leads the prospect through the process rather than depending on what the prospect wants to do next. (Prospects, more often than not, do not know what they want to do, and even when they do, they often do not know how to do it.) You need to know where you are going if have any hope of getting there.

A FEW KEY INSIGHTS WILL KEEP THE MOMENTUM GOING

Once the direction is defined by the map, you will need to create and maintain momentum. Following are the key items to remember when building momentum into your map:

1. Knowing what can go wrong at each stage of the selling process allows you to prepare for it and prevent it. The things that go wrong are consistent, and overconfidence is the biggest obstacle. Take preventative measures and have a plan to recover from anything that might go wrong.
2. Knowing what the owner of the alternative solution might do to derail the progress of the decision is a key foresight. You can set traps to lock competitors out.

3. Define the cadence of contact with each of the key players. Control and drive the process by keeping a cadence of communications with each of the key players in the account.
4. Set and hold a deadline that must be reached, and everything will be driven from this deadline.

Each milestone is important and needs to be understood properly. For instance, how do you know when you've achieved the technical sale or any of the other milestones? What will your competitors do once they know you have achieved a milestone? Remember, competitors in the space we're discussing (innovative or disruptive products and services) are competing for wallet share, but they are not competing on product or service because your offering is truly unique in the marketplace. Let's be crystal clear: Innovative and disruptive technologies are not incremental improvements; they represent a new paradigm altogether. The question then becomes how do we lead the prospect to the next step?

Also, what happens if you lose at a particular milestone? Do you give up and walk away? By no means. There are several tactics that you can use to recover from a perceived loss. You can try an end run to a higher power; you can muddy the waters with the weakest competitor.

THE RHYTHM TO REVENUE

Like everything else in life, a deal has a rhythm and a pace that need to be identified and followed. It is the salesperson's responsibility to lead the pace and to become concerned when the pace is broken. The rhythm needs to be established with each of the key players within the organization. Characteristics of the rhythm include the following:

1. You establish regular contact with the key players (the "let's talk next week" factor).
2. Commitment to the next touch point needs to be voluntary and mutually agreed upon.
3. If the rhythm is broken, it is a negative signal that needs to be addressed posthaste.
4. When a next touch point is not committed to, then you know that you do not have interest and you do not have an opportunity.

THE RULES BY WHICH A SOLUTION WILL BE SELECTED

Remember our key rule is "It is not the product." Who is it that sets the rules for selecting one solution over another? Well, it is usually whoever has the most compelling reason for selecting one versus the other. The C-player always blames the product, the company, the customer, and anything or anyone but him- or herself. It is the salesperson's job to define the reasons why a customer ought to buy his or her solution versus any other. If it were a pure matter of product superiority, then the superior product would always be selected, and there would be no reason to have more than one product for a market segment. But it is not the product; it is a collection of perceptions that are dynamic and changeable by talented mavericks. Think about the Recency Effect (the principle that the most recently presented items or experiences will most likely be remembered best). Viewers of two talented debaters will often flip-flop in their thinking each time the speaker changes. In the complex sale, what matters is not only what you are saying, but who you are saying it to and how often you are saying it. The rules by which decisions are made include such data points as the following:

1. Priorities
2. Values
3. Perceptions

A lockout is something only your solution has or does; beware of traps and remember the old saying: He who sets the rules wins the game. Set the rules.

THE POWER OF WHY

People will only do what they have a strong reason to do. So it is the salesperson's responsibility to establish the way for each of the players. It is also the salesperson's responsibility to keep reminding the prospect why they are buying, so the salesperson will always be prepared to give an answer to the question, "Why are we buying this product?"

1. Each person needs to know why they are purchasing.
2. Each person's reason can be different.

THE PLAYERS

Too often salespeople require a champion—or advocate—to do a lot of the selling for them. Having a champion is great, but you

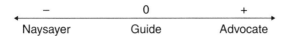

Figure 6.2 Technical buyer (end user) continuum.

cannot sell only to prospects that provide you with a champion. Moreover, you need to know how to sell *with* them, not under them. It is generally from the technical side of the house that you will find your helper. There is a continuum of support on the technical side of the house, and it is vital that it be understood.

The end user, or technical buyer, needs to be brought, at the very least, to zero. The positive end of the spectrum ranges from guide to advocate. So just exactly who are all these people? And who are the other players?

The Naysayer

The naysayer is the person who is going to block and kill the progress of the deal. He or she is generally the person who will lose power if your solution is selected. It is the person who feels it is his or his job to slow things down, and who feels that he or she must change the vision to add value. You don't need to make a naysayer into an advocate, but you need him or her to be neutral. Don't try to win the naysayer over—be satisfied with neutralizing him or her. Bring the naysayer to zero.

The Guide

The guide is not necessarily a great partner but is willing and helpful—as much as he or she can be. The guide likes what you have to offer and sees the value of it—but will not stick his or her neck out too far.

The Advocate

The advocate not only tells you what's going on but takes you to the economic buyer. He or she is your partner in the sale. Whatever the reason, he or she wants the sale to happen as badly as you do. The advocate helps identify the milestones, the rules, and the players, translates company-specific language for you, and provides insight into what the end vision must look like. He or she conscientiously warns of pitfalls and gives insight into the alternatives and what competitors are doing.

The Problem Owner

This is the business group leader who owns the problem that the maverick is trying to solve. The problem owner may not initially be aware of the pain he or she is suffering. The question is how do you get the problem owner to become aware of the pain that you can salve?

The Budget Owner

This is the person who will ultimately exchange money for a vision of the solution—how do you build up the value versus the cost? He or she will need a documented business justification. The budget owner is the one with whom you must share the bright and shiny vision of a future paved with gold, and who cries out for a visionary type of presentation. What is the end business result that will justify both the cost and the effort of making the change? The bigger and brighter the vision, the more it is worth. Extend the vision beyond the current functionality. You need to get budget owners to buy into not only what the product will do for them but how the business result will change them.

Selling without a Champion

We did not overlook the champion. With most descriptions of the complex sale, there is always a reference to a player who is a champion or someone who does a great deal of the selling for you. Some salespeople even go as far as saying that without a champion no one will be successful. We all know that when you have a champion, the process is a great deal easier, but a champion is not a necessity for someone who understands the process.

It is actually very dangerous to depend on any one individual regardless of his or her level of interest. Mavericks are their own champions, know the path that the decision will take, and build up the consensus of all the players.

SIGNALS

In sales, we are always evaluating what is happening within our prospect's account and what the true feelings are of each of the players. Too often sellers go by what is being verbalized by the players and ignore what is being left unsaid. The most accurate representation of what is really happening comes from the signals or actions that are being taken. The signals must be learned as quickly as possible, especially if you are losing to a competitor or to "no action required."

To control the process, you need to work with accurate and current information, so learning about and watching for signals is crucial.

Positive Signals

The following signals need to be validated to make sure they are true:

- Prospect makes and keeps a commitment.
- They ask for justifications, either technical or financial.
- They include you in internal meetings.
- They provide introductions to others.
- They share impressions of the competition.

Negative Signals

- Most questions are about an alternative's strength/traps/lockouts.
- The communication cadence is broken.
- Unexpected milestones are added.
- The advocate is losing credibility.
- The advocate's information is not helping.

Consider what the signals are that are unique to your product.

Integrity Scale

Tracking each player's integrity will give a way of gauging each interaction with him or her. Examples of such tracking include the following:

- How accurate is their information?
- Are they on time?
- Do they keep cadence with you?
- Are they selling you to get free product or services?

The power of the map to money is not in creating a mandated corporate process but in marking the pivotal milestones and decision points. Once you identify the pattern by which organizations determine to buy your product, you can match your skills to build your own unique strategy. It also needs to be said that your map is your own, and it can be on paper, built with a software application, on a whiteboard, or even in your head. The format of the map does not matter. The use and content of the map do matter. Without the map, your journey is touch and go, so—at minimum—think the process through and work with your peers to determine the best approach to each and every issue.

With long sales cycles and managing many opportunities, it is easy to become rusty or even neglect particular skills. The map gives you a quick refresher to the issues and variables that you are facing. Many people tell us that after closing a large deal, they feel like a fish out of water because they have not prospected in three to six months. The map gives people a feeling of leverage in that they do not have to recreate the wheel but can simply build off their experience of success and learn from their failures.

The typical representations of a complex sale only categorize the players or list the milestones of a deal. The map to money documents the whole picture and allows the individual to match the terrain and typology to his or her skills. The fact is that, without the map, we are relying on gut instinct and instinctive skills. With the map, there is a clearly defined process that has been proven to work successfully.

Chapter 7

The First Sales Call

BUILDING A VISION

Everyone knows the emotional energy and angst that goes into a first date and understands what the nervousness and threat of rejection does to an otherwise even-keeled person. Recall the difficulties you encountered on the first meeting when your gut told you that your date was not very interested in you. At that moment, you realized that it was all up to you to convince your date how great a person you are. Before the date, you rehearsed everything in your mind, wrote "talking points," prepared your funniest stories, and chose the coolest unknown place that would be a hit for your date. We all know that if we do not connect on the first date, our follow-up calls will go unanswered or we will be stonewalled with alternatives similar to the old standby "I need to wash my hair on Saturday night."

The first face-to-face sales call is much like a first date, and it is vital because too often it is the last sales call. The first call is the hardest because it requires the most preparation, the prospect cares the least, and most of the deal-killing mistakes take place. We spend a great deal of time on the first call because without a qualified and documented success, salespeople may be misled into believing everything is moving forward when, in truth, all they have is an illusion of a successful meeting. That illusion gives the salesperson a comfort feeling for weeks and months until the day that he or she realizes there is nothing.

Does it seem logical that someone would spend weeks working on getting the first meeting with a company and once the appointment is made only spend a few minutes preparing for the meeting? No, of course not. But that is what many do. They rationalize it by saying, "Hey, let's see what they have to say." The other problem is people spend too much time practicing their slide deck and collecting information packs, but they do not develop a strategy to describe the problems that their product solves.

In sales, like structural engineering, there is the "chain link syndrome." This is the description that was given when I worked for a company ironically named Chain Link Technology as the VP of sales described what happened after the first sales call. You could swap out the name Chain Link for pretty much the name of any company and it would fit into the syndrome. The syndrome was simple. An aggressive salesperson gains access to an account and builds enough interest to schedule a meeting. The salesperson, armed with a talented and prepared domain expert, arrives for a briefing. The presentation goes flawlessly, with several "wows" and "ahs." The demonstration of the product is received with great enthusiasm. The meeting goes far past the allocated 90 minutes, and the sales team leaves and gives each other high fives in the parking lot, knowing that they have knocked it out of the park and that it is now a forecasted deal. The salesperson follows up with a timely call one week after the meeting to confer and ask what they would like to do next. Unfortunately, the call and subsequent e-mails go unanswered, and it seems as if they had never had the meeting in the first place. So, what went wrong? The prospect was clearly interested and amazed at the presentation, but yet the idea died in the client's hands, and the sales company felt like this was something that had never happened before in the annals of business. So rare was the event that they called it a syndrome and warned all new salespeople that this is something that can (and will) happen. Well, was it unusual or was it the result of a lack of a sales process?

This syndrome is not a mystery to those who understand maverick salespeople and the difference between a complex and a simple sale. What was missing from this sales call was a way to connect to the next milestone in the decision path. Did the salesperson give each person a reason why his or her lives would be better because of the product?

You may be saying to yourself that it is so obvious they did not close for the next meeting or sense what the prospect wanted or needed. These problems are classic and affect the rookie as well as the 20-year veteran and can indicate the difference between the B- and A-player. The B-player is reacting to what the prospect wants instead of leading the prospect through the process of making a business decision.

Similar to the first date, if you do all the talking, the client, may be entertained but get lost in the meeting because you come across as self-centered. Maybe the opposite could work. Maybe by having questions that would show interest in the other person and his or her needs, you would get insight into areas of common interest.

The objective of the first call is to determine first whether the account is qualified, meaning that there is a need/pain that can be identified and built upon. From that point, you have something that can be developed and matched to what your product does. Much like the first date, you want to learn if you are interested in more than what you already know, which may just be an appearance. The balance of finding out what you want to know without offending or being transparent becomes the challenge.

The first call can come about in several ways, including a response to either a cold call or request for information from the prospect. We will separate the first calls into two main types of calls: a push, where the salesperson makes an initial phone call to build interest, and a pull, where the prospect has expressed interest in learning about the product. In the new market space the problem is that there are few pull calls, which makes it the salesperson's responsibility to gain the first face-to-face meeting.

The indirect approach of gaining a first meeting is a powerful technique. The indirect approach is to ask for an informational interview or a market research discussion. Asking for someone's feedback and insight is a great deal less threatening than presenting a product to sell him or her. These indirect meetings are low-key, useful in the qualification process, and serve to provide feedback on the real use of the product. Not so surprisingly, the informational interviews turn into experiential prototypes and even become the first customers.

A common analogy of selling in a new market is showing an ink blot and letting the observer share what value he or she gets out of it.

THE RORSCHACH ANALOGY

Anyone who remembers taking college psychology will remember being shown ink blot charts and asked what he or she sees see in the chart. The answers that people give to what they see gives the psychologist insight into the personality of the person giving the answers. Selling new products into new markets is very much like the Rorschach ink blots in that the seller expects new and varying responses to the use of his or her new product. The seller should embrace these reactions as long as the product is capable of adding value to the situation. Too often the seller, or, worse, the start-up company, defines a particular use of the product that is based more on industry analysts' projections than on real-world application. The communication of new products will naturally feel like showing an ink blot. The salesperson's responsibility is to build the emotional state within the prospect that will guide him or her to see immediate use for the product. The ink blot is a useful analogy because it forces the viewer to create his or her own meaning for the image, rather than simply equating it to a known image. What we can extract from the Rorschach approach is to not present the new product in comparison to an existing product, but rather as something completely different. The key is to preface the new product with questions that elicit the experiential pain of the current situation.

Let's use the situation of a cold call where you are pushing to meet with the prospective client. This call, like all calls, is best delivered one-on-one, where you are looking to magnify the pain that the client has and that your product solves. Once you have determined that the account is qualified, meaning that they have the need, you must ensure that they are participating and have the financial resources to complete a transaction. The need can be either discovered or undiscovered, but at the end of the meeting, without uncovering the need/pain, there will not be a deal. In the rare exception, there is a deal without a need that results from someone cramming the product into an unnecessary place where it will just collect dust, possibly engender bad will, and create poor future business relations.

When it is a pull call, meaning that the prospect is looking for a product and yours is one of the possible choices, this would seem like an easier sale. In truth, what is really happening is that the prospect has asked three or more of your competitors to demonstrate products, and this becomes a dogfight to see who wins. The prospect clearly views you as just one of many, so the job is to determine his or her real and perceived needs and to have your product and company match them to a significantly higher degree than your competitor's product or approach.

The prospect that contacts you with a pull call is not going to be a key player. Most often, this contact is simply there to orchestrate the meeting and administrate the logistics. You will need to push to get a face-to-face prep meeting so that the presentation will be a success. The person calling you is going to view your request as a hassle, so quid pro quo is the best approach as exemplified below.

The best execution of the quid pro quo is to agree with the prospect and say, "Yes, we look forward to making the presentation to your team, and before we schedule, may I have a 10-minute conversation with the lead technical person on the meeting team?"

You do not want to make the quid pro quo a condition; rather, it becomes simply a part of completing what the prospect has requested.

If they refuse your request, you can see this as a signal that you are not a critical option for their choice. Of course, you do not want to walk away, so an alternative strategy may be to do some networking and research to find the key technical player and contact him or her directly, using someone else from your company so as to not be seen as someone end-running the process.

Once you are able to get the prep meeting, it should be casual and one-on-one so that you can gather as much information as possible about the client's situation (need/pain) and end goals. You want to be sensitive to traps that your competitors have set and what would be in the key technical decision maker's best interest.

Once you have your presentation set, request a meeting with the key technical decision maker after the call to talk about providing some kind of value. This will be a key time to get his or her feedback.

Of course, the key test of how well the meeting has gone is if you receive a commitment for the next meeting. The best way to confirm the next meeting is to do it one-on-one in order to avoid the "we will get back to you" canned response.

The most important law that applies to the first sales call is that if you know what is going to happen, then you will know what to do. If your presentation and demonstration takes two hours and you only have an hour and a half, you will need to schedule two meetings (which is a good thing). Having met with a great deal of junior salespeople and questioning them about their first calls, you hear the same thing over and over: "It went great and they really got it." My next question asking when the next meeting is scheduled often elicits the same response: "They asked me to check back in a couple of weeks." At this point I realize this junior salesperson does not fully understand the process.

Recall the "chain link syndrome" at the beginning of the chapter. A great presenter can capture people's interest, but without identifying the need/pain and leading the prospects to understand how the product's capability will ease the pain, there is no compelling reason for the prospective client to move forward to a next meeting. If you know the prospect is not willing to commit to a next meeting or communication, you can be confident that you will not have a deal. So, if you know what is going to happen, let's talk about what we should do to make the good things happen and the bad things not.

Mavericks have a brutal sense of self-evaluation regarding where they stand in a deal and go so far as to set up acid tests for each position. The acid test for determining if you passed the first call is if the prospect commits to the next meeting or not. This momentum test is the most powerful test of where you stand. It is just too easy to say thanks for meeting with us and I will call you next week. This is a cop-out, and what is missing is the salesperson giving the prospect a need to return his or her call next week. The close for the next communication is, in a sense, asking the prospect, "What is in the way of us moving to the next step?" An important note is that if the account is not qualified, you certainly do not want to spend any more time or commit to a next meeting. If the prospect cancels your next meeting without quickly rescheduling, your deal is suspect at best.

Following is a list of how to tell if the sales call went well or if it was not successful.

The Good Things

Your product is seen as the best match.

The prospect has committed to a next meeting or communication.

You have set traps for the competitors who will present after you.

The prospect has asked for something, and you use quid pro quo for something in exchange.

The Bad Things

The prospect did not understand the value of your product, or did not "get it."

You walked into a competitor's trap and could not get out.

The prospect loved the presentation but did not commit to a next meeting.

You could not get one-on-one time with the key players.

You missed the signals.

The prospect did not identify the pain or did not see how you solved their pain.

Another law to remember when working on the technical sale is that the first call is not about the product. It is the art of identifying the pain that the prospect is experiencing that leads to setting the rules as to how the problem will be solved. The product is the crutch that the junior salespeople depends on and blames for all the bad things that happen. Mavericks take full responsibility for the deal, and doing so opens their minds to all the elements.

WHAT TO DO AFTER THE MEETING?

Unlike a date, your sales calls affect your income and level of career success, so they need a higher amount of examination and review.

The Postmortem

Early in my career I had the honor of working with a team of senior salespeople who were extremely successful and talented. One of their habits was to have what they called a postmortem after each face-to-face sales call. They would pick the meeting apart, write out the new information that they found, and update the organizational chart with changes of what they had discovered. This exercise was a way to continue building and refining their map. They would compare how this deal was working to several of the deals that they had done in the past. They would rank each of the players as to whether they were positive, neutral, or negative to the product. Working together as a team, the group would play a type of war game by asking what would happen if the sales group did either x or y and debating the best actions to take.

I learned more in those postmortem meetings than I have in any training class. By thinking through the issues and possible actions, the sales team could have a plan that everyone accepted.

After I left this company I was surprised to learn that other salespeople do not do this activity and it was not worth the time because the customer will either buy or not. We learned that even salespeople with 15 or 20 years of experience would not develop themselves beyond the interpersonal selling skills level and did not have a strategy. They would rely on their bubbly personalities or hounding prospects until they simply gave into their demands. However, as the sale becomes more and more complex, the skills are simply not enough; salespeople need to understand how the decision is going to be made, develop a strategy to convince each of the players that the decision means selecting your product and that it is worth substantially more than the money that they are paying.

After the meeting, as soon as possible, you need to sit back and review what took place. Replay their questions and the interaction that took place among the players. Use a sign-in sheet to make sure you have everyone's contact info and who was interested in what items. Label the player that seemed smart and interested and asked questions. The sign-in sheet is the most important artifact from the first call. Without it, you may have business cards, but not everyone brings business cards and the information on them is often out-of-date, making follow-up difficult.

Another smart move is to leave a couple of questions unanswered for the simple purpose of justifying a follow-up call. Again, if they are not interested in scheduling a time to get the answers to their questions, then you do not have a deal and that is what we call a signal.

The next law to apply is divide and "concur." If this is a pull call, it becomes harder to apply divide and concur because you are not talking to a problem owner or a player with power. The person you are talking to simply wants you to commit to a presentation.

After the first call, use the divide and concur approach with each person who was at the presentation. The different insights that you get from each will be valuable and will enable you to build a picture of what to do next and how to accomplish the tasks.

Think about how the law of divide and concur would work in the dating world. Would you really want to take your first date to meet your family or friends? Imagine managing your date's impression of you with your mother showing pictures of you in the bathtub when you were two years old or your friends sharing stories of your college years. Even worse, imagine having to be with friends of your date, who would all be qualifying you for how you would fit into their social circle. From this example, it becomes clear that convincing people is always most effective one-on-one.

After the first sales call, you will be able to identify the key players, including who is the most important and who is responsible for making a recommendation to the business problem owner. Consider whose opinion matters most and who are the naysayers.

How to determine if you are prepared for the first sales call:

- Do you understand with whom you are meeting and what they know about your product so far?
- What other customers do you have that have already done what your target prospect wants to do?
- Have you done Internet research on the company and the person with whom you are meeting?
- How can you apply what you have learned from your research to make the call more applicable to the prospect's situation?
- What are the typical things that the prospect wants from you and your company if the meeting goes well?
- What are the corresponding items that you can get in exchange?
- What traps may have been set for you by your competitors?
- What lockouts can you use to limit the impact your competitors may have?

Chapter 8

The Technical Sale

The technical sale is important but not critical when selling in a new market. It is defined as the selection of the innovative or disruptive solution to the exclusion of all other alternatives to solve a business problem. It is the winning over of the end user, the functionality evaluator who will actually have to use the new product or service to meet a real need. The good news is that many end users are also industry specialists who love innovation for its own sake, and they find themselves willing to adopt a new approach just because it is cool. The bad news is, of course, they don't hold the purse strings.

The technical sale in the new market space is very different in several ways and infinitely more complex than selling into an established market. In an established market there will be interest and pull, but that is all but nonexistent in the new market space. The level of resistance is very high in the new market space because any innovation will require a great deal of change to the buying organization and the value that the product brings has not been proven. The seller's job is to reduce the resistance by all means available and to increase the value at the same time. People who are used to only selling to others who already understand what their product does and the value it provides will be overwhelmed in the new market space. They will feel that it is the product's fault or that marketing has not positioned the value proposition correctly.

Without the new market selling skills and strategies, the sales team will quickly get disgruntled and give up. In the established market, the technical sale looks a great deal like a beauty contest without any rules, where there are a set criteria, a small group of judges, and a shrinking list of contestants. Here established market sellers are comfortable and skillful. These competitive skills will also be necessary in the new market once a need is identified and a vision is established.

There are three states of the technical sale: favorite, neutral, and not the favorite. The target state of favorite is the only one in which you will be given positive reinforcement and, therefore, the only state you will know for sure that you are in. Whether you are in the neutral state or in the not-the-favorite state, you won't know—so your job is, at least, to neutralize anyone who has not given you positive reinforcement. Each state requires a different strategy because they are all open to change and manipulation.

THE MECHANICS OF THE TECHNICAL SALE

Establish Yourself as the Favorite

The purpose of the technical sale is to create a smooth path to and validation of the business sale. It will also make implementation much easier if you have the end users on your side. There is no magic bullet for the technical sale; it takes hard work. If you are selling an innovative or disruptive product, you are apt to meet with resistance. People fear the unknown. They have ever since they believed the Earth was flat and it was possible to sail

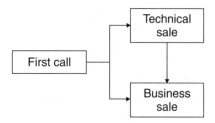

Figure 8.1 The process map at the highest level.

off the end of it. Fortunately, as we pointed out, many technical buyers are apt to be technologists who love innovation. You must generally convince your audience, the technical buyer, first, that he or she has a need and, second, that you can solve it—albeit in an unorthodox fashion.

Therefore, the steps through the technical sale are as follows:

1. Establish that there is something that needs to be solved.
2. Become a possible solution.
3. Become the preferred solution.
4. Lock out the alternative solutions.
5. Secure an introduction to the business buyer, the earlier in the process, the better.

Establish That There Is Something That Needs to Be Solved

With products that offer an incremental improvement, selling efforts are focused on the *product*. This is so much better, faster, cheaper, and so on. And the more familiar the customer is with the market space, the more obvious it is that it is just an improvement (an extraordinary improvement notwithstanding).

The problem is that with an innovation, selling efforts need to be focused on the *experience*. A new paradigm is often so far out of the prospect's frame of reference that unless you are dealing with a serious expert, the product by itself will make no sense. Imagine what it was like trying to sell an automobile in the early days. You could really sell it only as a hobby for the wealthy because there were no roads and people didn't understand the concept of machinery for leisure—machinery was for work. So if you were selling a car (versus the horse and buggy), you would have had to focus the potential customer on the experience. "Do you ever have to be somewhere at a specific time? What happens when it's raining and muddy? What happens when your horse throws a shoe?" You needed to keep bringing them back to the experience—not the technology.

So it is in the modern age when you are dealing with a disruptive shift. You must focus on the experience, not the product. Therefore, you have to frame the conversation with a problem that the end user probably doesn't even know he or she has. You have to convince the customer that there is a better way to do things and that the current way of doing things is fraught with *future* peril. You are here to save the customer from future disaster. It is in many ways a powerful skill. It comes back to painting a picture, sharing a vision of what the future could be—both positive and negative.

Become a Possible Solution

Once the technical buyer sees the vision and accepts that there could be a problem, you need to show him or her that your technology is a practical (compared to the looming danger), relatively low-cost solution. The prospect needs to understand that your wares will in fact meet the case and are a legitimate potential solution.

Become the Preferred Solution

Having established that there is a very real problem and that you have a possible solution, you must convince your technical buyer that you are in fact the preferred solution. You have an advantage in that yours is the only product in the running. But there will be competition from the status quo, and there will be competition for a share of the wallet from those who can meet today's immediate needs. Continue to build value by focusing on the experience—wouldn't it be nice to be able to visit your family 20 miles away in one hour rather than two?

Lock Out the Alternative Solutions

Competing ideas will arise, although there are no competing products—not for what you are selling. The lockout is that particular characteristic that is unique to your product or company—an industry standard, for example, or a patent, or a functional characteristic or support capability. It is that characteristic that sets you apart (and above) and that cannot be replicated by any other. It effectively locks out the competition. It is a very powerful strategy because it gives the customer a reason to select you, and you avoid having to compete on the myriad of other issues. Many salespeople are concerned that their lockout will not matter to the customer, but the point is that even if it doesn't matter now, it will matter in the future. With this in mind, you need to beware of one thing. In negotiations, it is called argument dilution: The lockout loses its power if it does not stand alone. Do not bring up a number of lockouts (even if they are all legitimate); it dilutes the power of your argument. Choose the one that will have the most impact and that best matches the prospect's particular situation. If the lockout is a technical lockout, it is important to map it to a business value so that once you are capturing the business sale, the businesspeople can understand what it means to them.

The inverse of the lockout is the trap—which explains to the prospect exactly why the lockout does not matter and is actually a bad idea.

LOCKOUT CASE STUDY

At Rational, a software company, we had a powerful lockout feature that we were able to use extremely successfully against our competitors. Regardless of the huge price difference between us and all the other alternatives, we were able to justify that higher price. Rational had a revolutionary capability to see the impact of a software change before you actually made the change, and once you determined that you wanted the change, you only needed to change the pieces of the software that changed rather than entire software application. This capability was called incremental compilation. Today, this capability may seem commonplace, but in the late 1980s, this was both a unique and a powerful feature.

This lockout was the key capability that we used because no one was even within years of having it. We were ruthless in building up the benefits of this capability by both showing the technical teams within the prospective accounts and building simple return on investment calculators to illustrate how each change would cost thousands of dollars and weeks of delay of delivery of new releases for the software applications.

The beauty of this lockout is that it has both a technical side and a business side, and as long as the salespersons were able to communicate both sides, they were able to win the deal. The most successful salespeople were able connect the experiential pain to not having incremental compilation. For the technical decision makers, it would make their lives simpler because they did not have to wait, sometimes for hours, to make changes. For the business players, the experience is how they felt about missing deadlines and the impact on their careers.

After years of winning huge deals away from all of our competitors, they scrambled to come up with weak imitations of this functionality, but it was too little and too late, and we were able to gain market share like a steam roller.

The Trap

Even in a new market, the competitive landscape becomes defined quickly and each competitor establishes its lockouts and knows its competitors' lockouts. The inverse of a lockout is a trap, which is either set for you to step into or left for you to set. If your competitor has been into an account before you and you know it, then you will need to make sure you do not step into the traps the competitor has no doubt set (assuming he or she is a shrewd competitor). If you are the first one into an account, you will want to set a trap for your competitor.

For example, standards are a typical lockout/trap item. There will be standards that you have and your competitor does not and vice versa. If you are asked very early in the call if you support a particular standard, then you know a trap has been set for you. Do not spring it. The best way to avoid a trap is to address the issue before it is asked, so that you have the opportunity to explain your position without being defensive and save the prospect the embarrassment of having to ask the question.

"Industry standards" is the most common trap that competitors set. It is a simple trap to set and can take hours of selling time to get out of. In the database, one of the standards that defined the use of databases was Structured Query Language, or SQL. If the competitor supported the language, then they would make it the most important requirement. In the early 1990s, the race to support the SQL standard was on, and it was the trap that the vendors who supported it used. The companies that did not yet support it would get stuck in the trap, and few could get out of it.

What will your competitors do once they sense that they are not the favorite?

The End Run

The end run is the strategy to go around the technical recommendation and straight to the business owner of the problem and explain why the criteria and rules are wrong. The unstated message is, "If you do not go with my product and instead go with the other one you are considering, the future of your company is in grave danger." It is an attempt to leverage the purse strings to force the technicians to reevaluate. There are a few proactive measures that can be taken to prevent the end run. First, prepare your contacts for the possibility that competitors will be bitter and may try something unfavorable to reverse their decision. Second, lead your contacts to explain to the competitors that the evaluation phase has been put on hold and it may take a great deal longer to determine which product will be selected. Third, have your contacts express positive feedback to your competitors as a way for them to avoid unwanted phone calls.

The end run is the key reason that it is so important to start the business sale as early in the sales process as possible. That way if you need to do the end run, you will have established enough of a relationship that you'll be given the opportunity to be heard. If you win the technical recommendation, then you will have the opportunity to warn the business players what is in store for them from your competitors.

Neutral (or Undetermined)

You most likely are in the neutral state of the technical sale when you are getting questions and you are receiving both positive and negative feedback. The good news is that you are getting news. In this position, you must follow the law of divide and concur because you will get the most accurate information from one-on-one interactions. This communication preferably takes place off-site, where you can learn about the rules and the power structure.

Dominate the prospect's time and establish deeper relationships on the business side so that you have a base from which to recover if things go awry. The strategies that work best on the business side are showing social proof that your solution is the viable approach for solving this particular problem. In addition, provide reference calls and, better yet, arrange a field trip to a customer who has implemented your product and would share why they purchased it.

The business side needs to hear the business reasons and why these reasons are so important. They are not interested in any individual technical feature that the competitors may have planted. The most dangerous thing about being in the undetermined state is that you are most likely not the favorite. And using the fundamental law that what is not overtly positive is covertly negative—well, draw your own conclusions.

Not the Favorite

How do you know that you are not the favorite? It's not as easy to determine as you may think because they are not going to tell you at first and maybe not at all. The signals will be that momentum is broken and calls go unreturned. You start to hear questions about the known competitor lockouts. The feature that was never a priority is now the most important requirement. Such signals should set off the alert bells.

When you suspect that you are not the favorite, there are several possible responses, which can be used in any combination:

- Get with the most positive player you have, and seek to discover what has changed and who is not on board.
- Get product management, even the VP of engineering, involved. They live the feature issue. Well managed, this will give the naysayer the opportunity to gain visibility and feel important by establishing a relationship with your company.
- Execute the end run.

When executing the end run:

- Don't ask permission from anyone to meet with the business owner.
- Bring in higher authority: The business owner will feel important and will be less likely to say no. (Bringing in the higher authority also gives you an out with the players you have a relationship with by simply blaming the higher authority.)
- Change the rules such that business issues trump technical issues.

Muddy the Waters

If the end run fails, the approach is to reset the rules. The "muddy the waters" strategy is to reset the rules and introduce new, weaker alternatives. By muddying the waters, you buy time to unseat the current favorite. To counteract the "muddy the waters" strategy, be prepared and set traps for the alternatives.

Reaffirm with your contacts why the rules are what they are. Warn the prospect about the possibility of a "muddy the waters" campaign being employed by your competitors, and remind him or her that it would affect the process and jeopardize his or her ability to meet the deadline.

Finally, let's take a look at the players who are typically involved in determining a technical recommendation:

- *The end users.* These are the people who will be using the product once it is purchased. There are typically just a few involved in the evaluation phase. They are challenging because each will have his own or her preferences that are often the opposite of everyone else's.
- *The naysayers.* These are the people who just have to approve your product or service. They care only about their niche in the company and will not use the product. An example might be the security group or standards monitoring group.
- *The leader.* This is the person who will make the final recommendation. He or she knows the issues inside out and will push you. The leader will delegate the work on evaluation to others who may try to expand the requirements far beyond what is really desired or needed.

KEEPING THE MOMENTUM GOING

With each key play, think ahead about three things that will keep the momentum going and be very concerned if momentum is broken. The momentum item needs to have a date when it must either happen, be canceled, or be rescheduled. Some ideas for keeping the momentum going include the following:

- Reference call
- Future product releases call
- Jointly developed presentation and demo
- Off-site coffee or meal
- Working together on an implementation plan

Building Your Map for Gaining the Technical Sale

It is time to apply what you have learned to building your own map to the technical sale. The first step is to identify the players who will be involved. The most important player is the technical leader, so think back to the deals that you have worked on and ask yourself who was typically the person needing to be convinced that your product was the right product. You also want to determine the roles of each of the players in the decision process.

Determining the milestones of the technical sale is the next step, which will give you the direction you will need to go. Again, review past deals and talk over the deals that your colleagues have completed to determine what the flow has been. Milestones that we have typically seen are presentation, custom demonstration, pilot, group demonstration of pilot, and jointly built implementation plan. Having many milestones gives you options to share with your prospects, and the more reasons you have for them to spend time with you, the higher the probability that you will get the technical recommendation.

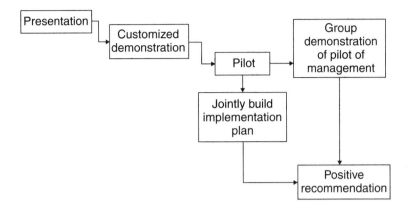

Figure 8.2 Sample view of the technical sale.

Once your map to the technical sale is drawn, as shown in Figure 8.2, you will have a sense of where you are, what is going to happen next, and what needs to happen next.

Chapter 9

The Business Sale

The business sale is having the prospect's irreversible commitment to purchase in hand, usually in the form of a purchase order or contract. The business sale is best treated as a separate selling effort from the technical sale because it is possible to lose the technical recommendation and still gain the business sale. It is true that very experienced salespeople may ignore the technical sale and focus only on the business sale. In fact, they can be very successful with this strategy, but they leave themselves open to getting hamstrung by a shrewd competitor who can team with the technical decision makers and capture the deal.

If the business sale is not started as soon as the technical sale, you will not have the relationships that will be needed in the case of losing the technical recommendation. Too often the business sale is not begun until the technical sale is secured. This is far too late and leads to false deals and to deals that take longer and become smaller. The business campaign should begin at the same time as the technical campaign, and the two should run concurrently. It is harder to work the business campaign because the business players do not know why they are dealing with you, not yet having decided to select your product.

Quid pro quo is the most powerful technique and should be used as the method to gain introduction to the person who will sponsor you from a financial standpoint. The technical players will always want something, and at the first sizeable request, you should exchange an introduction to the business players for fulfilling their request. A relationship will need to be established with the sequence of people who will need to approve the purchase. In each case—that is, individually—they will need to understand why they might approve your offering over the alternatives.

The biggest mistake salespeople make in the business campaign—after not working the business sale in parallel from the beginning—is not learning the language that the businesspeople talk. Businesspeople focus on the operations, execution, and leadership issues. They care about revenue, expenses, and the competitiveness of the business. They want to know how this purchase will affect these areas of the business, how it will impact the bottom line. They do not care about your product's bells and whistles, no matter how cool. They do not want to see demonstrations (which take valuable time), but they do want to learn about your company's suitability as a partner. And they want to know what experiences other companies like their own have had when they have used your product.

UNDERSTANDING THE DIFFERENT MOTIVES

The players in the business campaign are very diverse; they have very different motives and views. They do share a disinterest in products and features and a supreme interest in the business issues and outcomes your product will support, but that's probably about as far as the similarities among them go. Their interests are often political, almost always economic, and certainly financial.

THE SLIDING FORECAST

Every sales manager knows the sliding forecast. The sliding forecast is what happens when deals on the forecast slide from month to month and quarter to quarter. The salesperson does not really grasp it because the prospect says nothing but great things about the product and how badly he or she needs it. The prospect meets with you and shares information openly, but still the deal is not closing. There is always just one more approval required, and then it will be done. But the deal never gets done. It never closes, and the salesperson never learns what he or she is doing wrong.

The preeminent cause of the sliding forecast is the failure to recognize the fact that every deal has two major components—the technical sale and the business sale—as well as the corollary, which is that you cannot rely on a technical player to get the business sale. This is true for several reasons. The technical player may not know how to help you win the business, and there's a good chance that he or she has no experience with the buying process in his or her own company. Moreover, the technical player does not want to lose the help and support that you've been giving and doesn't want it to end. The junior sales rep is also more comfortable talking with the technical players because they are more accessible and they have the product in common.

Salespeople tend to be optimistic. One of our salespeople said a deal was worth $1.7 million. I asked, out of curiosity, "Have you met the guy who's going to foot the bill?" "Well, no," came the timid reply. It turned out to be a $100,000 deal.

Recall the case in Chapter 6 of the 15-year-old boy going into a Porsche dealership and whose father comes in just as the salesman is readying the paperwork for the deal. The technical buyer, like the 15-year-old Porsche shopper, does not have financial decision-making authority. He cannot write the check. He must take you to the economic, or business, buyer. The business buyer, by contrast, is likely to take you to the technical buyer to see if your product actually works. He has political, financial, or user experience, but not technical experience.

The junior salesperson tends to focus on the product's functionality. He or she may be very successful in convincing the technical decision makers that they absolutely must have his product. But the salesperson is likely to fall flat when it comes to getting the business sale because of several issues:

- First, the junior salesperson is naive enough to believe that getting the technical sale is enough and that the technical players will naturally get the business sale for him or her.
- Second, it is a rare salesperson who will be capable of speaking to all the issues of the different players that will be involved in any deal. The good news is that they will not have to. The strategy of pulling in their own executives to speak with their counterparts at the prospect organization is always wise. The business players need their issues addressed and their questions answered. When a junior rep talks to them about features and functions, the business player rolls his eyes and starts to think about his next meeting. Here, as with all player interactions, the first law comes into play: Everyone will ultimately act in his or her own self-interest.

- Third, in many cases the technical players do not want you to gain access to the business players. This is an area that you need to manage very carefully. It is a real and dangerous sign when the technical players are blocking you because it can mean that they have not yet briefed the business players regarding what they are doing, or most likely, they do not want to lose control over the decision. They also may see it as unnecessary and see no value in introducing you. So it is very important to build trust. But once they ask for something, it is time to request an introduction and possibly pull in a higher authority from your organization so that the business sale can begin.

WHAT CAN GO WRONG IN THE BUSINESS SALE?

The biggest mistake salespeople make in pursuit of the business sale is the failure to supply the key business player with a compelling enough reason to meet. The business players need to have a strong reason to meet with you, especially early in the process, lest they view you as just another salesperson looking to rush a decision and end-run the technical due diligence. The business player's natural tendency is to buy as little as possible, which is, of course, the opposite of what the seller wants.

THE BUSINESS PLAYERS

- *The business unit managers who own the problem that your product is solving.* They typically will not have the spending approval for the total amount needed, so they are not the final economic decision makers. Their creditability is critical because without it, you will be on your own to convince the final decision maker.

- *Everyone above the business unit manager, up to the final signature on the purchase request.* How high you go in the organization will depend largely on the amount of money that you are seeking. Typically, anything above $50,000 will require a vice president to sign, and anything over $100,000 will require the president to sign. Often when a purchase exceeds $1 million, it will require the board of directors. The approval of the purchase will depend on the size of the organization and how long it has been in business. Your business player most likely will not know this process or the timing of it, so it is up to the salesperson to determine.

- *Any necessary legal approval that will depend on the contractual requirements that your company and the prospect's company require.* This process can be simply an administrative process and just take time, or this can be a real deal killer. The process needs to be managed to make sure that all your work is not wasted. Any deal killers that come up in the legal phase should be addressed from the beginning of the sale to determine whether they can be overcome.

- *All necessary purchase approval, like the legal approval process or the purchasing group process.* The purchasing group will want to add value to the company by trying to get additional discount. It is very important that you have support from a power player for the prospect so that when you speak to the purchasing representative, you can explain that the discount has already been pushed to the greatest it can be.

THE NATURAL SALES LAWS THAT APPLY TO
THE BUSINESS CAMPAIGN

- *Nothing happens unless you make it happen.* The business sale will not happen without someone driving it. Certainly, the internal technical recommendation will help start the business sale, but someone needs to explain the business value and write up the justification. If the salesperson leaves it to his or her internal sponsor to do the business sale, the risk is increased and control is reduced. If the salesperson drives the business sale, he or she controls the process and can direct it in his or her favor. By providing a draft business justification with the formal technical recommendation, you have the framework to build a formal justification that can function as a mutual project to work on.

- *Everyone will ultimately act in his own self-interest.* Knowing that everyone will do what serves him or her best will do two things for you: First, you will know what they are interested in, and second, it will explain what they will ultimately do. The maverick seller will test the words that each player uses versus the actions that he or she takes. Everyone knows that it is the player's actions that matter, but we often get distracted by the words that the player says. When you constantly review the actions that the player takes, you will get a better sense as to what his or her words really mean. Our judgment can also be clouded by our own best interest. Our need to close the deal is our interest but not our prospect's. We need to remember and concentrate on what is in the prospect's best interest and sell to it.

- *What is not overtly positive is covertly negative.* At the business sale, if you are not getting consistent cooperation and feedback, then you need to recognize that something is wrong and you need to correct it. When you have a technical sale, there will be a need to continue with the momentum because the natural reaction after the technical sale is for the prospect to ask whether this product makes business sense for the company.
- *It is not the product.* For the business sale, the important discussion is not what the product can do but the impact the product will have on the business. The topics that the business players care about are financial and political, not functional.

WHAT TO DO IF YOU DO NOT GET THE BUSINESS SALE

Regardless of the success with the technical team and the business owner of the problem, getting money from any organization is always a challenge. The proposal can make great business sense and have a short return on investment, but you always need to be prepared for rejection or delay. The fallback or plan B should be prepared so that momentum is not completely lost; your plan B should, at a minimum, commit the prospect to your company's product. By committing the prospect to your product, you will have the prospect as a customer and will have the opportunity to continue the selling process. If the prospect does not make any financial commitment to your product and just says that the company needs more time, this will greatly reduce the likelihood that anything will happen.

THE BUSINESS JUSTIFICATION

The most powerful tool to capture the business sale is the business justification. This is a document that is developed jointly with the prospect. Having a draft of a business justification that you can customize to each particular prospect is critical for success. Technical players will have to prepare some kind of a report on their due diligence, so if you can give them a framework, you are solving two problems at once. First, you are helping the prospect get his or her work done. But second, and more important, you are framing the justification on your strengths. By working on the justification jointly with the prospects, you are getting a lot of face time—or at least e-mail communication—which will give you greater insight into how the organization works and how to develop your strategy. And because the technical players are unlikely to know how to build a business justification, they will need a great deal of help.

The business player will typically be required to write something up as well, and your draft business justification is a great fit for this need. The business justification outline that follows will help you structure a successful document that can be presented to senior management and board members, justifying the need for a purchase.

THE BUSINESS JUSTIFICATION OUTLINE

I. Executive summary
    1. Outline the history of why the technical evaluation was done and what business problems it will solve. The

executive summary should be only a couple of paragraphs and should be targeted at the final business player from whom you require approval.

2. The proposed solution: Describe at a high level the recommended solution that focuses on solving the business problem and not just the product.

II. Requirements

1. Talk to the business issues that are problems today and are costing the business. The costs need to be outlined and described.

2. Keep in mind that they can be current costs or future costs.

III. Alternatives

1. Discuss the competitors that were evaluated and why they did not meet the decision criteria. It is very important that a detailed and fair evaluation was completed and your product was the only viable solution. This part is best if you write it so as to have the most detailed description of the alternatives and then let the prospect review it.

2. It is important to lock out everyone else completely so that the door is closed behind your solution.

IV. Evaluation process

1. Talk to the process that was used for evaluation; it is key to explain the depth to which they went to make the selection.

2. Make sure every possible question is answered and every issue is raised.

3. Develop a table of requirements, and have your product as the only one that meets all of the requirements.

4. Include reference calls that have validated that your product has been used in the same type of situation.

Recommendation: Describe in detail the recommended approach that maps business requirements with product and implementation issues.

V. ROI (return on investment)

1. The most important part is the ROI because the ROI justifies the money that is being exchanged for the product. If the ROI is done well, the prospect will view the product as an investment versus an expense.

2. The business players want to know what they are getting for their money and how long it is going take to get their investment back. The ROI should be worked on jointly and project a payback in less than one year. The ROI should include both cost reductions and revenue increases.

VI. Implementation plan

1. You want to show that you have thought through the issues beyond just the purchase and have a well-thought-out plan to implement the solution.

2. You need to show what it takes to make the product successful, including the costs and time frame.

VII. Schedule

1. The schedule sets the deadline for getting to the fulfillment of the vision and is the date that the prospect cares about.

2. Provide a date for each step and an owner; working backward will drive each needed decision. These dates will create and maintain the momentum; the timeline will bring awareness, which will cause the need to take action.

3. The date that you care most about is, of course, the purchase order, which will define the achievement of the business sale.

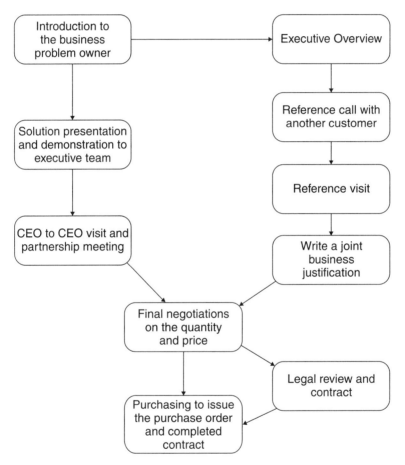

Figure 9.1 Sample map to the business sale.

Chapter 10

New Market
Selling Strategies

William E. Rothschild asked, "What do you want to achieve or avoid? The answers to this question are objectives. How will you go about achieving your desired results? The answer to this you can call strategy." That is the sense in which we are discussing strategy. Strategies are skillful maneuvers for successfully executing the selling process. This is an area on which few sellers focus enough attention. Salespeople are typically looking for the magic words that will make the sale, that will make up for a lack of characteristics, skills, or a strategy. There are no magic words. It takes knowledge, practice, and discipline. But the good news is we have found that the smarter and more consistent approach is to take what you already do best and apply it to the selling process. That is, your unique talents, properly applied, can work.

When people try to learn new selling skills, they often become overwhelmed and end up sounding phony and incongruent. We have found that the most effective approach is to figure out what you do best, the skills that come naturally to you, and base your strategy on those skills. You must, of course, master the *process* in which the strategy plays. If you do want to expand your repertoire, to add more arrows to the proverbial quiver, then practice just one skill at a time until you master it.

BASIC STRATEGIES
Relationship Building

Relationship building is the most common selling strategy and the most recognized skill of talented salespeople. Of course, if relationship building was enough for successful sales, there would be a lot more killer salespeople. But this is strategy without a complete understanding and command of the process. It is often said that people buy from people they like or, more to the point, from people they trust. It is true that people will do more for people they like and enjoy spending time with, but if a competitor knows the *process* (i.e., how to position his or her product and lock yours out), the players could be your best friends, but they will not buy from you. Relationship building is only an effective strategy in the context of process.

Steve was the master of the relationship-building strategy and very successful as a salesperson. He was a very nice guy and a pleasure to speak with—really a joy to be around—but he knew that people didn't buy from him because of his personality. Steve was aware that it was his skill at relationship building that gave him insight into organizational needs and how clients felt they could best solve these needs. He would have breakfast with one of the several guides he had befriended in an account to catch up on what had happened since the last client meeting and to help his guide with any issues he may be facing, reassuring his guide that he was there as backup.

Steve was difficult to manage: He was never in the office and was always late with his forecast and expenses. But he was always welcome to all of his prospects and customers. He understood intuitively that because no one bought from him at his office, he needed to be out there in the field building relationships. He realized that if he was not connecting with each key player in a prospect organization, then his competitor would be.

Steve was bold—which is not to say brazen. He would make dinner plans with the CEO of each of his prospects for the purpose of getting them away from the office and learning what really makes them tick. He was very careful never to use these opportunities for a sales pitch but rather to gain insight into what these CEOs cared about, what they were focused on, what kept them up at night. Steve's colleagues accused him of hobnobbing, relying on his charm and his expense account to close deals. But the truth is that Steve had mastered the strategy of relationship building. He had discovered the secret of reading people correctly, knowing when they were being straight with him and when they were brushing him off. Steve mastered the relationship-building strategy and leveraged it to create a new market.

Product Passion

Another common strategy is to be passionate about your product and enthusiastic when presenting it. Enthusiasm is very contagious. This strategy will certainly help you with the technical players and is very powerful in gaining the technical win, but it won't work with the business players. Business players are looking for business results and outcomes. While they may appreciate your passion and enthusiasm, they will not be swayed by it.

Product passion and enthusiasm tend to be the domain of end users and their ilk. These are rare traits among typical salespeople, but they can make for powerful strategy. Henry was an engineer-turned-salesperson. He brought to sales a very unusual mixture of deep technical knowledge and skill and an ability to see and describe the unique value of a product in relation to business outcomes. His transition from engineering management to sales was born from frustration with the sales organizations' apparent inability to communicate product differentiators to prospective clients. He had held the profession of selling in somewhat low esteem, based on a general sense that salespeople are overpaid and underskilled. Now he was one of them and determined to show himself better than the rest. Henry was a master at the presentation and demonstration, but at first he was unable to connect with a customer's pain or see what might drive that customer to the next stage. He was brilliant with the technical win because he could always wow the end users, but it took some time to learn that each buyer in an organization has his or her own language and really cares about the product only to the extent that it adds value to his or her role within the company.

Then Henry teamed up with a manager who taught him to distinguish between the technical win and the business win. Henry's passion and enthusiasm covered a multitude of sins while he learned the skills that make for great sales. His drive and intellect also helped to make up for the foibles. Now his passion and enthusiasm remain unabated, but they are under rein and used strategically.

Account Entry Point: Two Strategies

There are typically two ways to approach and enter an account: bottom up and top down.

Bottom Up

This strategy is used when the salesperson initially approaches the end users of the product, the people who are experiencing the pain or might see a need for your innovative or disruptive technology. Here, you gain the technical win first and then work your way up to the decision makers.

Top Down

This strategy is to enter the account at the business player or senior executive level with a strong business case for the use of your product and then use executive support to work with the technical players.

We have found that both of these strategies work and that neither is necessarily preferable. Some sellers use one; some use the other. It is really a matter of personal preference and comfort level. You should use whichever you're most comfortable with. The thing that separates the maverick from the B-player is that the maverick actually uses one or the other as a strategic maneuver and does not just work with prospects that come through the leads produced by marketing.

ADVANCED STRATEGIES

New market sellers have developed several advanced strategies that are teachable and repeatable. Anyone can learn them and put them into practice. They are not difficult to master, but they may require some internal selling. Most companies are not pre-disposed to handle these strategies for their salespeople, but we've never worked with a company that wasn't willing to at least listen to new ideas regarding selling. Indeed, every company wants to be successful, and most are crying out for leadership in how to close more deals.

"We're All in This Together"

This is a very powerful strategy that works particularly well with very large deals. It is most applicable to the new product/new market sell. This strategy brings to bear the full resources of the selling company. Of course, this strategy does not scale to all of the salespeople of even a mid-sized firm, but for one or two salespeople, it can be incredibly useful. This strategy is the best and highest use of the divide and concur law as applied to inter-nal as well as external forces. It involves matching the players in your own company with their counterparts in the prospect com-pany. For example, arrange for your VP of engineering to meet with the prospect's VP of engineering. The power of this strat-egy is twofold. First, it is an excellent example of how to keep the momentum going. Second, it gives the prospect a comfort level and a sense that he or she is important. This strategy reduces risk.

Karen is a experienced new market seller. She is not a master of product knowledge nor particularly interested in the details. Her colleagues tease her about never having gone on a sales call alone. But this is not in fact a weakness; rather, it is her great strength and talent. For Karen is a master of the "we're all in this together" strategy of sales. Karen has built enormous trust internally—with her colleagues, her managers, and even her CEO. They trust her and are eager to support her because she only brings them in strategically—where they can bring value—never as cannon fodder. She always seems to know precisely who would bring the most value to a client meeting—and inevitably shows up with that person: always the right person at the right time. She knows her own strengths and her weaknesses and augments them with key players. She would describe her style as a deal manager rather than being a lone wolf.

Again, it is always strategic. It is never reactionary or responding to a crisis. Karen doesn't just bring people along for the sake of companionship or backup. Karen always has a plan for how a colleague can contribute positively to the progression of the sale. Karen can do the work of three salespeople because there are always others working with her clients on her behalf. And by leveraging even her CEO, she is able to get meetings others would never dream of arranging.

The "we're all in this together" strategy requires a great deal of coordination and preparation and is dependent on the interpersonal skills of the people that you bring into the account. There is nothing worse than bringing in an executive who does not have solid communication skills or team-building skills or an executive who appears to care more for her own success than the success of the prospect. So, the first questions you have to ask yourself are these: "Who are the players that bring value to the sales team? Who will benefit the relationship, exuding the right impression, rather than be a detriment?" Everyone has war stories of bringing in a manager or an executive who steps in it or puts his foot in his mouth, causing weeks of repair work to get the process back on track. So before finalizing the team, poll your colleagues and find out how potential team members have done in the past in front of prospects. You must set the team up for success.

As a new market salesperson, you want to control the process from beginning to end. Set the agendas for the meetings; guide your executive in what to do and what to say, and more importantly, what not to do and what not to say. Here's an example of what can happen if you don't prepare for every contingency within the realm of the possible: Some years ago, I took a customer out for a fancy steak dinner and made the mistake of inviting my unprepared and unrehearsed manager. As we were bonding over cocktails, the customer was explaining how his company was building its future strategy on one of our products. My manager chose this moment to point out that, in fact, we were canceling that product from our suite of offerings. Well, imagine how that went over. I quickly explained that, while true, we had a replacement strategy and would continue to support the product well into the future. But my manager kept on down the path of how our company was going a different direction. He just wouldn't stop. It was a train wreck. I kicked him under the table, but he just didn't get that this was not the time or the place to drop bad news. This was the time and place to take the opportunity to learn more about what our customer was looking to do and figure out how we might partner together for mutual benefit. I take partial responsibility for the gaffe. I should have prepared the manager in advance, suggesting that there might be a more appropriate time to share the news about our evolving product strategy. But, really, who could have imagined that an otherwise experienced sales manager would say something so negative over cocktails?

"Refuse to Lose"

This strategy is, precisely as it sounds, refusal to allow a loss. It requires excellent interpersonal skills that will allow you access to the players who have already decided not to move forward with you. Obviously, even expert sellers lose sometimes—even the best lose deals—but the best never give up. You can do everything right, but people are people. They are unpredictable. And there are always new and unexpected players and competitors. The new market seller treats it all as opportunity.

Now it may seem to be more of an attitude than a strategy; it is both. It is certainly the most consistent belief system that we have noticed among the mavericks we've studied. Refusing to lose keeps the focus on the end goal every day and keeps the salesperson focused on the fact that it is his or her responsibility to win. The characteristics that define the "refuse to lose" strategy/attitude are determination, persistence, and the belief that each deal is winnable.

A powerful example of the "refuse to lose" mentality comes from outside the sales arena and touches the hearts and minds of anyone who remembers it. On September 11, 2001, United Flight 93 was hijacked. It was the intention of the hijackers to crash the plane into the United States Capitol or possibly the White House. The Twin Towers and the Pentagon had already been attacked on that fateful morning. An Oracle salesperson, Todd Beamer, and several other maverick passengers had learned what was happening from their loved ones via cell phone calls. That day they stepped out of their roles as ordinary airline passengers and into the roles of heroes. They refused to lose. Winning meant not allowing the hijackers to win. They decided that dying passively and doing what they were told to do were not acceptable; it was simply not going to happen. They banded together, risking their safety and possible death, to recapture the aircraft from the terrorists. They chose to refuse to lose, to win control over their destiny. They fought for their lives, took the control away from the terrorists, and changed the course of history. They did not allow the hijackers to complete their mission. They could have sat back in fear and let things take their course—but not on their watch. They rose up taking control of their destiny and refused to lose. This is maverick thinking at its best.

This strategy must be used throughout the process, not only once it becomes apparent that you are not going to win a deal. The sooner you sense that you may not be winning, the sooner you can adjust your strategy. Remember the law: "Whatever is not overtly positive is covertly negative." B-players will walk away the moment they discover they lost the deal; they will turn their attention to other opportunities. Mavericks will not give up so easily. They will work with their guides in the account to understand what's happening, who's behind the selection, and what rules they are applying to justify the decision. The maverick will then determine whether the player who is pushing for the competitive product can be converted in order to decide whether to use a direct or indirect strategy.

There are those who believe that once you've lost a deal, any continuation is throwing good time after bad. But those who can execute this strategy often are able to regain quickly deals that others would pass by.

So what exactly is the "refuse to lose" strategy, and how do you execute it? It takes iron will and great confidence but also finesse to break down the lockout that has been put in place without appearing rude or unconscionable. It can be done in any number of ways, from the end run to the sharp price cut. The point is that you simply refuse to lose, and by persisting, you win the deal.

"The Kingpin Strategy"

We have alluded to this strategy in earlier chapters, but this strategy is so powerful that it deserves a deeper explanation. The kingpin strategy, when executed well, makes selling so much easier. The strategy is to identify the kingpin within a territory and do whatever it takes to win that account. Then use the kingpin reference and case study to win the next tier of accounts. When leaders move in a direction, others follow. There is nothing more convincing than a rave review from a market leader. This strategy requires an experienced salesperson to be able to build the connection with the kingpin— which is likely a difficult account to penetrate. More-junior salespeople will focus on the low-hanging fruit instead. The problem with low-hanging fruit is that each deal is tactical and independent. Without the kingpin strategy, you are not really building a business.

Kent was the talented salesperson who taught us the kingpin strategy. He was very creative and very meticulous; he never made a move without first working out a strategy. Kent had been selling to the federal government for about 10 years when we met him. He was a real student of government organization and the interdependencies of the different agencies. He made it his business to know the lay of the land so well that when he figured out whom the kingpin was and made the sale, the rest of the agencies would fall in line like dominoes. His whole approach, in fact, was based on the domino principle, and so his strategy was developed with the endgame (falling dominoes) in mind. He developed his presentations to describe what the world would look like when the entire government was standardized on his product. He leveraged every evaluation—and even every positive meeting—to move closer and closer to the kingpin. When he finally arrived in the kingpin's office, after only a year, he was able to capture the entire federal government as a client in one fell swoop. It actually forced his own company to change its business model in order to meet the needs of his large array of new customers.

The mistake that some people make with this strategy is working only on the kingpin—and no one else—until the kingpin is won over. The great thing is to work all the angles and leverage every available resource. The new market sellers understand that the kingpin will take time and patience. Work on those near the kingpin as you formulate the strategy and line up the dominoes. But always keep your eye on the prize. Kent used every opportunity to build a groundswell of interest and support so that when the kingpin finally made the purchase, all the pieces fell into place.

171

"It All Comes Down to One Thing"

This strategy is about finding the one reason that a prospect *needs* to purchase your product now. This was a common strategy with the new market sellers we studied. It may seem simple, but it can be challenging to determine what the one thing actually is and how best to position it. The power in the "one thing" strategy is that all of the players will have a clear understanding of why they are purchasing the product. Typically, the "one thing" is a lockout feature of the product that matches to a financial benefit. The "one thing" can be technical for the technical users and financial for the business players—they don't all have to be sold on the same thing. The key is to find that single reason that will sway each player and link it to the end result.

At Rational, we had the ultimate "one thing" feature, and it gave us market supremacy. It was a functionality that worked as a lockout almost invariably and allowed us to be extremely successful against our competitors despite the enormous price difference between us and every other alternative. Rational had developed the revolutionary capability to see the impact of a software change, without actually having to make the change. That is to say, it allowed you to see what was going to happen with each change you made to the system and therefore allowed you to pinpoint those changes that had merit. It then allowed you to make specific, targeted changes without changing the entire software application. Today, this capability is commonplace, but at the time, in the late 1980s, it was a unique and game-changing feature.

We hammered this "one thing" lockout capability relentlessly because no one else was within years of having this capability. We would wow the technical teams in prospective accounts and build simple ROI calculators that showed business buyers how each change by a competitor would cost thousands of dollars and weeks of delay on the delivery of new releases of software applications. It appealed to both the technical end users and the business buyers, allowing savvy salespeople to communicate with both sides and win the deal. After years of winning huge deals away from all of our competitors, they scrambled and came up with weak imitations, but it was too little, too late. We gained market share like a juggernaut, all based on the strategy that it all comes down to one thing.

"Let's Be Partners"

This strategy is most powerful when coupled with the kingpin strategy and the "we're all in this together" strategy because the only thing better than winning the kingpin account is joining the kingpin as a partner. Partnerships are desirable on any number of levels. The customer will have influence into the future product direction and gain access to the new features before they are generally available. Moreover, the customer will want to ensure the success of the product so that their investment is protected. The value to the seller is in both the obvious financial reward and, from a marketing standpoint, the partnership bringing tremendous credibility.

Mike had a slightly different approach that leveraged both the relationship strategy and the "we're all in this together" strategy to create a strategy uniquely his own. He would, in essence, "marry" the customer to his own company. He would get product development at his own company involved so that his customers' requirements would make it into the next version of the product—and any problems with the product would be fixed in a timely fashion. Mike's marketing team would work with his customers' marketing teams to create success stories and joint advertising. Mike was able to lock out the competition by making his customers feel like family. Why would they possibly look elsewhere to have problems solved? He would even have the CEOs of all his customers visit his own corporate headquarters to meet everyone and get a sense of the future direction of the company. As it happens, Mike was able to get three times the revenue from his customers than any other salesperson.

As the partnership broadens and deepens, it will bond the two organizations. A partnership is the formalization of the quid pro quo law without the ping-pong nature of quid pro quo on each item. The typical mistake in the partnership strategy is not formalizing it and then not executing it. The partnership should include sales, product development, support, and marketing, not just sales. When properly executed, the partnership strategy might include joint ad campaigns, site visits with key prospects, product feedback, and enterprise-size purchasing.

"I'm in Control"

It's true that it's hard to control other people, but it is possible to control the process. The first step to controlling the process is understanding the process. Without control of the process, you are simply reacting to the prospect, and those reactions are just too late to win the deal. You may feel that prospects do not want to be controlled—and you would be correct—but what they do want is to be led. They want to be led because they are on new ground and do not know how to purchase your product. They also most likely do not understand what needs to be done to complete the administration process of purchasing. This is why controlling the process is so critical. The how-to is not hard, but it is not really explained or taught by sales training courses. The courses that we have studied focus only on the one-on-one, single call and explain that the larger complex sale is just a collection of small simple sales. This is just the tip of the iceberg. Without understanding the process and without having a strategy, you are on a treasure hunt without a treasure map. You are not in control.

There is a major difference between the A- and B-players, and it is simple to tell the difference. First, you can ask, "When is your next meeting with the prospect?" The B-player will say, "I have a call in to the prospect and should hear back soon." The A-player will give you the date, time, and place. Not getting a commitment to the next communication is a negative signal that there may be some covertly negative item that is not being shared. You need to dig deeper. The only legitimate reason for no specified future communication is that you did not propose a good enough reason for the prospect to meet or join a conference call.

The other part of control is momentum: The deal in motion tends to stay in motion, and a deal at rest tends to stay at rest. Without momentum, you do not have control because you will spend all your time trying to create momentum. Other than always arranging the next communication, momentum can be achieved by the divide and concur law. When you keep everyone focused on the deadline to receive the benefit of the product and then list all the items that need to take place, it will create that sense of urgency. Watching for any signal that momentum is slowing is vital. Once you sense slowed momentum, immediate action is required because there are two reasons for a change: Either the customer has a higher priority or the customer is moving forward with another product. Neither of the other reasons is going to help you, and you need to understand quickly what the cause is and come up with a strategy to get momentum back.

"The Ecosystem"

This strategy is very powerful because, although complex, it is repeatable. In every market there is an ecosystem that includes product companies, service companies, and recruiting companies. Within this ecosystem, the salesperson leverages everyone else who is working within a prospective market. The salesperson uses the natural interrelationships and interactions with the environment to bring the full extent of the system's resources to bear on his or her prospective client.

Our friend Ed was the master of the ecosystem strategy. He never did cold calls, and he never begged for a first call. Instead, he would build a network of all the product companies within a sector (his target market) and would then partner with the leading consulting companies that were targeting the market—and anyone else who he felt might be able to add value to the selling process, for that matter.

After having won several deals, Ed noticed that his customers were always looking for design tools just before they evaluated his product, so Ed met up with the leading design tool vendors in his territory and explained the value he could provide them. Ed would point out that he would share leads and would give endorsements to accounts that they were both working on. This partnering with other salespeople gave Ed more opportunities than he could handle.

Ed also met with the leading consulting companies that would implement not only his product but several others. Ed would determine the best and most professional people and then explain that he could also provide tremendous value by getting them work, asking only for an indirect reference in return. When Ed would meet with prospects, he would bring a complete solution to the table. Prospects inevitably felt that Ed understood their situation infinitely better than any of the other vendors. He was able to bring additional resources to the opportunity that solved problems that the prospect had—and not just the problem that his own product solved.

Part of the informal arrangement with the network of people and companies was that they would not share information with competitors and would not work with any of the other competitors. This is the risk inherent in the ecosystems strategy. These partnership relationships are not at the company level but at the personal, one-on-one basis. Trust is the key ingredient. It must be explained and committed to—with the knowledge that if the trust is broken, the arrangement will be ended. Ed would work with people who would also work with his competitors, but he was aware that whatever he said would most likely be shared with his competitors. He would rank his network of partners and would work it in the order of value.

Another of his tactics was to work with recruiters to move people who would not help him. The recruiter would call the accounts and competitors to get situational information and get them to interview with other opportunities. The recruiters would also help his prospects get the best people available. When Ed would be blocked and could not find any way around a particular person in the account, he would get his recruiter partners to pull that person out of his way. Ed was also great at managing the partners to make sure they did not know each other or how Ed was gaining such insight into the market and account knowledge.

"Baby Steps"

Island Exchange was a completely high-tech exchange that traded energy and other commodities all over the world—and all online. They were disgruntled with a current software vendor that they had built their exchange on because, now that they were growing, they felt that the vendor was taking advantage of them. The vendor knew that it would be expensive to replace its product with any other, so it was not at all flexible on the licensing and pricing.

Enter Jean Claude, who sold a competitive software product that was priced aggressively but was not yet as mature, nor was it robust. Jean Claude was the master of the baby steps strategy. He had worked for several start-ups and was a smart salesman who knew how to work against seemingly insurmountable odds. As with most of the leads that Jean Claude received, the one from Island Exchange was not valued very highly because the inside salesperson did not feel that the prospect was serious. It already had purchased a competitive product, and in this market, it was very hard to swap out products because substantial investments were made in learning and development.

Jean Claude knew better. He had done this at several companies before and knew that it is not only possible, but a fun challenge to win a deal from a competitor. The first call was set, and of course, there were no key decision makers there, and the focus was on a broad set of issues that spanned both the technical and business issues. The engineers who were assigned to the meeting had no business power but spent their time wanting to know licensing costs and future support cost—giving Jean Claude the clear impression that they just wanted to use him in the negotiations with their current vendor. Jean Claude deflected any cost questions, explaining that there are lots of variables and that much more understanding of what they wanted to do it on and on what types of hardware was needed to give an accurate view of the costs. He also gave the blanket statement that his company never loses on cost, as a way to deflect giving a cost answer to people who had no budget authority.

At the close of the first call, the usual request for an evaluation copy was brought up. Jean Claude agreed, noting that all he needed was a quick introduction to the CIO (who was the final technical decision maker, and whose name came up several times during the call), who had not attended. The engineers said that the CIO, Martin, was a very busy man and that he does not like to meet with vendors until his team has approved the product. Jean Claude smiled and said he understood and that he would just need five minutes of his time. He also said that his VP requires a meeting with the CIO as part of their process. The engineers reluctantly walked Jean Claude to the CIO's office. Jean Claude then explained how well the meeting went and that he would like to understand from the CIO why he is currently in the market to evaluate his product. Jean Claude worked in a lockout by explaining that his product was an implementation of the new Java standard and that their current supplier was not and would not be for years. Island Exchange had made the switch to the Java standard as a way of leveraging new technology and increasing the productivity of their software development team. The introduction went well, but there was still no clear signal other than that they wanted a proposal that the CIO could use as a negotiations tool against his current supplier.

On the way to the office, Jean Claude's manager called and wanted to know how the meeting had gone and, more importantly, whether they were serious about the idea of switching products. Jean Claude explained that he saw an opportunity in that he had a follow-up meeting on Friday that week to begin the evaluation process. It was a stretch, but he knew that if he told his boss how hard it would be, his boss would have pulled the plug and asked Jean Claude to work on some other opportunity.

Friday that week, Jean Claude did not bring his product but wanted to understand their current use of the existing product. This frustrated them because they simply wanted to install it and say that they had done their due diligence, but Jean Claude knew he wanted to drag this out (i.e., baby-step it as a way of building interest and gaining a deep understanding of how they were solving the current problem). By his not bringing the product, there was another quid pro quo that was available to

Jean Claude at the end of the meeting. If he had brought the product, then it may have been his last meeting with them. The original meeting was set for an hour, but Jean Claude kept pulling in more and more players and, at the end, suggested that they go to dinner to talk over the process and get a stronger feel for whether Jean Claude might have a better solution. Jean Claude was able to pull out of their usage of the other product problems that they saw and issues that his product could solve. He knew that he would have to change the rules so that he could gain an advantage beyond price.

Jean Claude was able to build relationships with several of the engineers without threatening the powerbase. He gathered enough information to build up a concept of substantial pain with their current solution and evoked two lockout features that Island Exchange bought into. Unfortunately, he ran into several major technical issues with both the product and its perform-ance. The situation was shaky at best and was like a rollercoaster over several months. After one particularly knotty meeting between Jean Claude's president and the CIO, the president remarked on the way back to the airport that he was wasting his time because the prospects hated them. Jean Claude, however, knew that if they were wasting their time, Island Exchange would have kicked them out by now. Thus, they continued their work with the product. Within a month, it was the end of Jean Claude's quarter, and he needed a deal to make his number, so he met with the CIO who held the IT budget and presented the business justification for the switch to his product. After several heated negotiations and many sleepless nights, a purchase was approved. Jean Claude's president was amazed—certain as he was that Jean Claude was pouring good money after bad. But Jean Claude knew what he was doing, and he knew how to take what everyone else thought was impossible and make it possible.

Jean Claude shared with us that the easiest way to keep a deal alive and moving forward is to keep taking small steps forward, or baby steps. These steps are so nonthreatening that no one can really object to them, but before they know it, they have come to the conclusion that your product has great value and you are a trusted member of their team. Larger steps require larger decisions. By breaking the decision into smaller decisions, risk for everyone is lowered. From a selling standpoint, this is the simplest strategy to learn and apply because there is not much technique to it other than asking for the next step and knowing what type of step can be taken without scaring anyone off. The baby steps strategy is often confused with relationship selling, which is building a relationship with the client and hoping that when the client needs the product, the client will purchase it. The baby steps strategy is based on understanding how organizations purchase but knowing that the situation is so difficult that it will require much more background work and new ways to position the product.

* * *

These are not the only possible strategies but just a small sample. Each salesperson should build his or her own unique approach based on his or her own skill set, ask for feedback on what areas need to be improved, and pick one skill a month to work on.

Chapter 11

The New Market
Sales Matrixes

The new market selling matrix is an array of the characteristics, skills, and attitudes that salespeople either have or need to develop. In Table 11.1 we have separated these skills into groups and put them in the order that they should be understood and developed.

Table 11.1 The New Market Selling Matrix

Characteristics	C-Player	B-Player	A-Player	Maverick
Proactiveness	Follower	Takes responsibility	Knows what to do and does it	Leads both the team and prospect
Intelligence	Is not intelligent or does not apply it	Understands what needs to be done	Knows the product and the market	Applies his or her intelligence to win and outsmart the competitors
Motivation	Does as little as needed to get by	Wants to be in the top 20%	Wants to be in the top 10%	Wants to be the best
Competitiveness	Feels prospects will do what they want	Likes to win but does not take it personally when he or she loses	Very competitive and needs to win	Extremely competitive and winning is the only thing
Creativity	Just does what he or she is told	Follows the company process	Creates new ways to close the deal	Determined to find a way to win every deal

WHAT'S IN IT FOR ME?

The beauty of a matrix like this is that it provides a basis for comparison and differentiation, both against the standard and against others—some of whom may be substantially more successful and, therefore, worthy of emulation. People are notoriously bad at self-analysis and can rarely pinpoint those attitudes and behaviors that actually make them more or less successful as compared to those behaviors that they *believe* make them successful. The skills shown here in the matrix are those that make people increasingly more successful. Mastery of them all makes one a Maverick. The matrix gives you a sense of what each level of player does differently and what separates them.

To determine what attitudes each player has about the major components or elements of selling, use the matrix as a guide. Learn the basics first and master them. The payoff will be immediate and considerable. The biggest mistake made by salespeople who are stuck in the land of the B-player is thinking that they already know the best way to sell and are already doing it. They don't, and they're not.

Look for a moment at Table 11.2, which shows the attitudes of the different levels of players. Make an honest assessment and decide where you fall—and then decide whether selling is really your passion. There is nothing worse than being in the wrong job.

How does a chef determine the quality of a particular dish? How much weight would he be likely to give to his own opinion or that of an underling? Probably not so much—as he would be unlikely to get useful, objective feedback. He is more likely to

Table 11.2 The Attitudes of Different Types of Players

Attitudes	**C-Player**	**B-Player**	**A-Player**	**Maverick**
Money	Pay the bills	Make target income	Leverage accelerators	Make the most in the company
Competition	You win some; you lose some	Knows how to work around them	Hates to lose and fights for every win	Marginalizes the competition, refusing to lose
Product	Depends on the product to sell	Knows how to position the product	Understands that it is the end result of what the product brings	Focuses on the end result of the business result the product brings
Territory	Territory makes the man	Depends on the quality of leads	Prospects without leads	Self-reliant and is successful regardless of the territory
Emotional Attachment	Detaches him- or herself from the results	Takes some responsibility	Owns the result	Takes total responsibility for winning and losing
Work	Work to live and not live to work	Career-oriented	Passionate about what they do	Selling is their profession and art form
Learning	As needed	Know it all	Hungry to learn more	Passion for learning every possible distinction
Motivation	Keeping their job	Making quota	Being in the top 10%	Being the #1 producer
Quota	A baseless objective	Objective to be met	The goal to be beat	The minimum bar to be crossed ASAP

seek the opinion of his colleagues and the general public who are the ultimate arbiters. And at what point is the master chef likely to say, "Well gosh, this is good enough!" When? Never. He is always seeking to improve on his own work. He would seek out the work of others whom he considers better than himself and find ways to integrate some of their ideas into his menu. He is always trying to raise the bar. So it is with the passionate sales-person, the maverick who is always seeking to improve his reper-toire. He seeks the opinions of his colleagues and his superiors; he thrives on feedback and coaching because he knows that he cannot see his own swing. He actively seeks the opinions of others to keep himself honest and objective.

By way of extending the cooking analogy, we must add that great chefs like new market salespeople are not born. They are made. The man who does a mean burger for the family on the backyard grill for the Fourth of July does not generally rise to the quality of gourmet chef at a four-star restaurant. If he aspires to be a great chef, he must build his repertoire skill-by-skill, dish-by-dish, burger to steak to lamb chop!

THE MATRIX FOR THE LOWER TIER

If you are a B-player and do not aspire to be an A-player, do not give your manager this book! Managers will quickly learn the limits of the B-player and will be on the hunt for the mavericks.

C-players are of course unlikely to be reading this book, but if you are, run and hide. The gig is up. Run, do not walk, to the nearest exit. If you are a C-player—and happy being a C-player—quit blaming everyone else and either get engaged or find some-thing that excites you enough to get engaged. You will be found out sooner or later. You are but a placeholder and will be replaced. Either get in the game or get out. You have it within your grasp to grow and develop. Do not stagnate. Do not give up. Get in the game. C-players are the first to be fired and the last to be hired. The C-player has really two options: decide that selling is what they want to do and to build or rebuild their skills or find another career path that better fits their skills and motivations.

Unlike selling skills, the new market seller's strategies and processes are off-field activities—you can learn them in the privacy of your own home. You don't have to practice in front of live prospects, with all the awkward stumbling about that usually entails. Indeed, when learning a new skill, sales often drop slightly for a short period while you get your sea legs. You will initially appear incongruent and stiff; you will be outside your comfort zone—but the payoff is fairly quick and well worth the trouble

By practicing the skills and strategies before and after your calls, you will begin to get a better sense of the lay of the land: where the deal is, what you need to do next, and what might go wrong. Once you have incorporated the method into your sales style, you will have a framework to use, adding a sense of logic and reason versus the conventional treasure hunt method.

HOW TO MOVE FROM BEING A C-PLAYER TO A B-PLAYER

Reviewing the distinctions between the C- and B-player is the place to start, and it is clear that the major differences are in the attitudes. If the C-player has the base characteristic of intelligence, what is typically missing with the C-player is motivation to change his or her view of selling. The key attitude that needs to be changed is being emotionally attached to winning, which will have the C-player take responsibility for winning the deal. With the two pillars of selling success being intelligence and motivation, the seller will have the foundation to learn what is needed and the energy to make it happen. If the seller does not have the minimum intelligence, he or she will not be able to learn what is needed. The good news is that even with the minimum intelligence level and a large amount of motivation, the seller will be able to push themselves to adapt to the environment. The most common cause of a seller being a C-player is just a lack of motivation to push them to the next level.

HOW TO MOVE FROM BEING A B-PLAYER TO AN A-PLAYER

Moving from a B-player to an A-player requires much more than the transition of a C to a B. The characteristics must be there, but they are just not enough. The A-player has developed powerful skills that take years of practice and determination. The B-player who wants to grow and develop will need to first admit that his or her skill set needs to be developed. The trap that most B-players get stuck in is that they already feel that they are A-players. The B-player is easy to identify because their response to any coaching or new approach is that they will describe in great detail that they have seen it all and done it all. B-players are close-minded and their own worst enemy. The obvious way to tell whether someone is an A-player or not is to see if he or she is able to produce the results consistently quarter after quarter. Often, a B-player with a great territory will get great results, and the B-player will grow to believe that it is his or her skill and not that he or she has been given the gift of a great territory. If the B-player can reflect on his or her abilities and ask for feedback, the B-player will learn what his or her weak areas are and put a plan together to develop the skills to get to the A-level.

With the majority of the salespeople falling into the B category, there are plenty of examples to examine what they do differently from their more successful peers. Managers like B-players because they do what they are told and are faithful workers. Within larger established companies, being a B-player is enough, and the B-player is seen as the desired team member. The challenge that the B-player will face is that if the company gets hit by a rough economy or an aggressive competitor, the B-player is outmatched. In the new market space the B-player is a fish out of water, and it will become clear very quickly. They will push their company into a stalemate position where the B-player is not willing to change to be successful. In the job market, the B-player will also find it hard to differentiate him- or herself from the herd of B-players.

HOW TO MOVE FROM BEING AN A-PLAYER TO A MAVERICK

Once the foundation of skills is integrated into the seller's personality, the difference between an A-player and a maverick becomes their unique strategies. Mavericks will implement their own strategy, but like the great chefs of the world, each carves out his or her own niche. A-players will have developed the maverick skill set of building a vision, setting direction, maintaining momentum, and controlling the process, but they will then need to develop their own strategies that raise their talents to the maverick level. Mavericks will be smart enough to know what their strengths are and strong enough to examine their weaknesses as well. Two of the general characteristics that separate A-players from mavericks are the creative or independent thinking and radical approaches to winning deals. Mavericks do not limit themselves to corporate structure or the prospect's protocol. Mavericks redefine what is allowable and possible; they break through the limits. Some people simply do not have the creativity to define their own strategy, so they adopt the strategy of another maverick.

THE MATRIX FOR MANAGERS

From a manager's standpoint, the matrix is a useful tool for ranking their own team and for evaluating interviewees. If managers can properly rank their team members, they may begin to understand why they keep missing the forecast and losing deals. They may gain some insight into the personnel changes that would make them more competitive in the new market selling environment.

Managers will gain great value by teaching and implementing the new market selling skills and strategies. Doing so provides a common language and framework and, thus, facilitates communication. A process map, customized to your particular product, will help you know where to spend coaching time and will pinpoint where you actually are in relation to the potential closing of deals. It will also massively improve your forecasting accuracy. See Tables 11.3 and 11.4.

The manager of C-players has been frustrated for quite awhile, unable to prod them to move and make anything happen. C-players work only on the deals that are pulling them; they do not prospect or work on developing dormant accounts. The manager's question about C-players is simple: Would we be better off

Table 11.3 New Market Selling Skills Matrix

New Market Skills	C-Player	B-Player	A-Player	Maverick
Vision Creation	Does not get it	Compares their product to existing approach	Can establish it with some but not the key players	Able to build the vision with everyone in the decision path
Direction	Natural course	Follow the process	Push and pull	Set and lead
Momentum	Follow the customer	Driven by the quarterly deadlines	Has momentum with one or two players	Creates and maintains momentum
Control	The customer is in control	In control when the prospect wants something	Control is gained and lost as the deal becomes more complex	Controls the process from beginning to end

Table 11.4 The Stakeholder's View of Each Player

Stakeholder	C-Player	B-Player	A-Player	Maverick
Customer	Vendor	Company's representative	Advocate	Team member
Manager	Dead weight	Solid contributor	Dependable	Rainmaker
Company	Burden	Company man	Rising star	Magician

having no one in the position? In most cases, they are better off, but barely. The managers will be looking to upgrade the position as soon as an opportunity presents itself. The mistake managers make is trying to change C-players. They do not want to change. They are burnt out, or they just don't get it, or they're in the wrong job. If you are stuck with a C-player, try to move him or her to a position that will have the least negative impact possible.

Managers of B-players can quickly determine whether the B-players can grow into A-players by judging whether, first, they think they know it all. Managers know when they try to coach the B-player and just get smiles and nods. B-players who feel that they know it all and have done everything possible already do not understand what they are missing and are not taking responsibility. If B-players are confident enough to examine their skills, acccept feedback, and recognize that they have room for improvement, the manager can coach them with the distinctions that would take their selling to the next level.

Managers of A-players typically just count their blessing, but there is still considerable room to grow. When the A-player is competing in a new market with a new product, the A-player will find it challenging, even when competing against other A-players. Managers in very complex and highly competitive markets will need A-players to rise to the maverick level. The good news is that A-players want to be better, so management just needs to coach them and support them. By practicing the skills and developing their strategies, A-players can quickly rise to the maverick level.

The different views of the players reveal some very important distinctions and explain, again, why there are so few mavericks. It becomes apparent that customers value the maverick seller more than the company the maverick works for. This is easily explained in that the customers see the value that the maverick brings to their businesses and sense the difference that a maverick seller makes. The company that the maverick works for may have in-fighting by less successful salespeople and managers to rationalize the maverick's success. The internal squabbling will be focused on saving face and diminishing the individual contribution of the maverick, so the internal perspective will likely be muddied. Your natural reaction to this internal selling environment might be, "If the maverick is successful, a great salesperson, why doesn't he manage the internal representation of his work as well as the customer-facing work?" Well, one characteristic of mavericks we have studied is that they shun the internal politics and thrive on the closing of deals. Frequently, the company does not know what to do with mavericks. If they have the proper political support, unique positions will be created for them, and both the maverick and the company will prosper.

Chapter 12

When the Maverick Seller Needs to Move On

When the mission of creating and capturing the new market has clearly been accomplished, an interesting side effect often happens. Inside the sales organization, instead of seeing an increased recognition for the maverick sellers, you will actually see that the perceived value of a maverick inside the organization is reversed. Now as the company becomes the market leader and the 800-pound gorilla to be dealt with, the company transitions into the hyper-growth phase of its life cycle. Instead of the problems associated with a sales organization fighting for each deal, the problems the organization faces now involve managing and maximizing the amount of pull it is receiving from the market. The selling skills that are needed are quickly migrating from battling for each transaction to managing many transactions and making those transactions larger and expediting them through the process.

The market has now been established, the product is known, and its value is well understood. The company quickly moves to an execution and operation organization and the tolerance for uniqueness and outside-the-box rebels is all but eliminated. Structure and systems are the focus to implement the uniformity needed, and the conventional method begins to fit perfectly.

Even the C-players are selling deals and appear like they know what they are doing.

The mavericks continue to be successful, but they feel trapped by the structure that has been sneaking into their daily lives. The management is no longer overlooking the lack of administrative reports that are expected, the updates to their forecast and firm adherence to the company's expense policy. What was once a great match has now turned into an uncomfortable union.

All the things that attracted the maverick seller have been diluted and may have even disappeared. An interesting dilemma exists in the sense that maverick is still doing well and the situation may not be painful enough to leave, but it turns into a slippery slope for both the company and the maverick salesperson. Each side of the equation becomes more and more a mismatch, degrading the level of effectiveness. The maverick encounters a new sales management that has no appreciation for his or her talent or contribution. The new management does not have the patience for the lack of organizational structure and the rebellious attitude of the maverick. The new management team sees little marginal value for the mavericks because they see the corporate-citizen B-players closing deals of equal size and volume. The new management does not dig into the deals to understand the cause and does not really care; they only care about their own situation, and the maverick has not been seen as enhancing it. The new management team is from the conventional, operations-oriented model and sees the challenge as administration with no need for any artistic skill. These are the exact people who would kill an innovative company, but yet they are now a necessary step to take the company to its next growth stage—becoming a mature industry leader. This will inevitably become the norm. Now the maverick has become the one who does not "get it"—even worse, they do not want to get it.

The challenge at this point becomes either to end the relationship without bad blood or to create another maverick-worthy opportunity within the growing organization. The company may have a need to create new products that target new markets that will require their talents. The risk to the company from a maverick leaving should be clear. There are starving competitors that would kill for the market leadership position, and who better to make that happen than the person who created the market? The dominate position in the market was created by the maverick and can be changed by the maverick. In adapting to the changing tides, the runners-up in the market segment can change the rules and win the game, so a maverick's value transcends the current situation. All of a sudden, the loss of the maverick has a significant impact far beyond the quarterly revenue number and touches on the core of the business as a whole.

MAVERICK MANAGEMENT CASE STUDY

When I first met Jack at the typical new-salesperson training class, he appeared scatterbrained and even burnt out. He had a fantastic track record of success at his previous company. I knew that his new manager was not yet convinced that Jack was a keeper and thought that he might not even make it through the next quarter. At the evening group dinners, Jack would show up late and appeared disheveled, as though this was the first time he been in a restaurant. Several of the other new salespeople had seen this happen before when a bad hire took place, and it even seemed comical. Jack's behavior continued, and the concern expressed by several members of the executive team also increased, but it was too early to make a decision on Jack.

After the first quarter was over, Jack had closed the first deal that was over $500,000 in less than 90 days, and the sales team regrouped for the quarterly sales meeting. The other salespeople all had their justification for Jack's success and their lesser performance. Part of the justification for Jack's performance was that he had inherited the deal and that it was not completely his efforts that generated the deal. Jack was feeling very happy with himself at the meeting. Each of the salespeople was required to prepare a presentation that reviewed the previous quarter and the outlook for the next quarter. Jack's presentation was attended by the president of the company and several other executives, but Jack's prowess with PowerPoint, the presentation software, was less than proficient. In fact, his slides looked like a first-grader had done them, and his presentation was characterized by his manager as embarrassing. The president shook his head and walked out of the room.

The second quarter was even better for Jack, with two deals that added up to over $900,000, about 30 percent of the start-up's revenue. Jack's success continued to give him a pass to behave any way he wanted, but his manager was getting frustrated with cleaning up after Jack and wanted to have Jack follow the company's selling activities, which included making a set number of sales calls per week and maintaining a sales plan for each forecasted deal. Jack ignored his manager and felt that the manager did not add any value to his selling efforts. Jack was correct in his assessment of his manager, but he was still his manager and he needed to work with him.

The first year was a very successful year for Jack, with a $2 million deal in the fourth quarter that knocked the ball out of the park. Even the president of the company became a Jack fan and cut Jack even more slack. Jack was a classic maverick. He was completely independent and could not articulate what he did to close these amazing deals.

The next year, the market exploded, and the company did what every company does. The CFO was very concerned that Jack was making more than anyone else in the company and that the company could hire five salespeople for what it was paying Jack. The $2 million deal had occurred the previous year, and there were new and higher expectations to meet, so the company cut Jack's territory and raised his quota. Jack did not feel valued for his contribution but liked the product and his prospects for the following year. The first quarter was a bust for Jack. Not a single deal was closed, and he was once again looking more like the idiot and less like the savant. Jack's manager continued to push him into selling the way he wanted him to and adhering to the company's administrative standards. The friction built to the point where Jack would not return his manager's calls. Jack wanted to report to the president of the company and work on the large deals that he liked to work on.

After Jack's second quarter that resulted in less than $50,000 of revenue, Jack's manager had the case built to have Jack fired. The memory of the first year was not enough to keep Jack afloat. Of course, the three people who took over Jack's territory did less than a quarter of the revenue that Jack had done, but they did keep their sales administration plans in order. Jack was not missed, but his revenue certainly was.

Often the successful company will be in the process of being acquired or going public. Either alternative brings along with it a great deal of change and turmoil. The acquisition of the company will bring many issues, depending on the acquiring company's objectives and perception of the need to retain the sales force.

With an initial public offering comes a new level of oversight and reporting that raises the level of visibility and transparency the company must now provide. The side effects of the new changes extend to all of the groups within the organization. Within the sales organization, the individual compensation will become a concern if a few people's income is disproportionately higher than the norm. Quickly, the logic will shift from a "whatever it takes" attitude to one of "if we pay one person $500,000, why can't we get five people and pay each of them $100,000?" The focus turns to profitability versus growth.

The need for maverick-level salespeople does not go away regardless of the size of the company, but as the company gets larger and larger, the tolerance for unique or special treatment becomes increasingly lower. Regardless of market share, there is always someone out there trying to change the rules and redefine the market place.

The approach that larger companies can take is the "skunk works" approach. For example, at one of the largest technology companies, they created a start-up within their large organization. Everything was separated but the administration functions. This move allowed different rules to apply to each of the groups so that they would be able work in the way they needed to compete in their marketplace. They could hire their own level of salespeople, with their own compensation plans and stock options. If the separate group had been required to use the existing sales organization, it would surely have failed because the new product required a new set of skills. This strategy has worked before but requires strong leadership that can keep the larger parent corporation from losing faith.

SKUNK WORKS

In the 1940s, Lockheed solved the problem of keeping its maverick engineers motivated and productive by separating them into a small group, which they called Skunk Works. They had control over their own staff, style, and budget. This radical approach was actually not just kept separate but also secret. Kelly Johnson, the leader of the group of the Skunk Works team, was the strong leader who was able to select his team and had the freedom to execute his vision. Johnson was able to deliver the advanced aircraft and the supporting technology in a fraction of the time and within a smaller budget.

Few companies can execute the skunk works strategies successfully, and we rarely have seen it done well. The other common approach is that a larger company will acquire a smaller company with a successful product. The thinking is that with the larger sales force and customer population, the new product can just be plugged in. This approach often fails because the acquired product has its own market and competitors, and having an untrained or junior salesperson compete for a customer against someone who sells only this product does not work. The acquiring sales management team most likely does not have experience managing mavericks. The larger companies are largely populated with B- and C-players who can skate by just selling more and more to the install base.

Managers who are unable to create a challenging and interesting opportunity for the mavericks on their team will find letters of resignation on their desks. The only thing worse than the resignations is having the mavericks growing more and more disgruntled. The managers need to find new situations for the mavericks to use their talents, which can include teaching less experienced salespeople or targeting new market segments.

There will be cases in which the maverick becomes such a mismatch for the organization that he or she no longer has a place within it. Such a situation is unfortunate but must be dealt with quickly and fairly. Mavericks will have no problem finding a new opportunity but may need the push to make it happen before the situation sours further. The most important problem to prevent is having the maverick go to a competitor where he or she can teach the skills to an army of salespeople hungry for market share. It is the manager's responsibility to give the maverick the support in finding a new, noncompetitive opportunity and to support the effort with recommendations. When done well, the exit will be graceful, without anyone being bitter or resentful.

Expanded Case Study

F
ollowing is the innovation and disruptive case study of Object Design Inc.

BACKGROUND

Object Design, Inc. (ODI) was a database company founded in 1998 by Tom Atwood and a small team of engineers. Backed by A-level venture capitalists and an executive team to match, ODI believed it would be the heir apparent to the next generation of database technology. ODI focused on storing software data in its actual form, rather than in rows and columns, as relational databases do. The company believed that the database market would evolve away from the relational model and into the object model similar to how the market evolved from hierarchical databases of the 1960s and 1970s to relational databases in the late 1980s and early 1990s. ODI was not alone in seeing this market opportunity. Quickly several companies, including Versant, Objectivity, Poet, and Ontos, were funded, and first releases of products were brought to market. This market developed into a classic disruptive market requiring not only competing against the incumbent players like Oracle and Sybase but also in-house solutions. One of the authors had the honor of being part of the sales team that helped create the market, starting at ODI in 1993 when there were about 60 employees. Those were heady times. Although it was still several years before the advent of the technology boom of the late 1990s, employees fantasized about what their stock options would be worth if they could have an Oracle-like market capitalization.

ODI is a compelling sales case study because it is a classic case of a new, innovative, and disruptive technology trying to create a new market. In the high-risk/high-reward environment that exists in the technology space, a pattern emerges. Once the venture capitalists see their counterparts finance a company, they quickly want to finance a company of their own and not miss out on this new opportunity. Soon several companies become capitalized, and the race is on. Products come to market within months of each other, marketing teams copy each other's messaging, and the sales teams are hired. From a customer's perspective, the products look the same. In this situation, the customers were also new to the space and had not thought out all the contingences. All too often the defining characteristic of the winning organization is the quality of the sales organization. The ODI case study is interesting because of what was believed to be at stake at the time: The lucrative software market was going to transition to object databases and the dominant object database company would own this space.

THE SALES TEAM

Evaluating the situation and the opportunity at hand, ODI realized that it needed a very talented group of salespeople to win in this market. The initial sales team that was recruited consisted of very experienced and successful people who had created markets before, and each had experience winning against tough competitors. The sales culture developed into a highly aggressive and competitive one, both for revenue and career advancement. The VP of sales had a strong understanding of the selling skills that were required. He did not do what most would have done—hire database salespeople just because ODI was in the database space. The first salespeople would have to have experience in highly competitive situations and know how to get both the technical sale and the business sale. These skills were in high demand, and the company did not have time for the salespeople to learn them on the job. The team that was assembled was as good as any and well suited to the challenge.

Knowing that the sales would be highly competitive and that revenue was desperately needed to fuel the company, the senior salespeople were given the freedom to do what was needed to win the deals. All too often sales leadership likes to enforce a structured process that has worked in an established market where there is a standard process that the prospect goes through. The other issue was that these senior salespeople needed to have the freedom and independence to do what they know best; they would not tolerate lots of reporting or oversight.

EARLY SUCCESS

With its highly skilled and aggressive sales team, ODI was able to capture several very high profile early adopters, including NeXT, Sun Microsystems, and IBM. All of these early adopters were valuable for their revenue, as well as for positioning ODI as the technology and market leader. In 1994 *Inc.* magazine named ODI the fastest-growing company, making ODI number 1 on its Inc. 500 list, growing an amazing 23,376.2 percent in just 5 years. From the outside, the future of ODI was a sure thing—and Oracle better look out. What the outside did not know was that half the growth in 1994 was from one customer, IBM, who prepaid about $12 million dollars in run-time license fees. Run-time licenses were a lot like music copyrights. When a company wants to include a songwriter's song in its commercial or movie, it is required to purchase a license to do so. Similarly, ODI's database was being built into other people's software and a license fee was paid. Since the salespeople were only paid for revenue received, they were highly incentivized to get these run-time fees paid in advance regardless of the loss of long-term margin to ODI. ODI wanted the license fee as soon as possible to accelerate the growth rate and to fund the expansion of the organization. It was this run-time license business model that made winning this market so attractive—but eating tomorrow's dinner today would eventually catch up with them.

THE OBJECT DATABASE MARKET

Regardless of the wishful thinking of the visionaries, this market was different from the relational database market and completely new. One of the early mistakes was positioning object databases as the next generation of database technology. This was a mistake for two major reasons. First, it required that object database have at minimum equal functionality to relational databases. Second, the relational database market was an established database market rather than a completely new and separate market. The object database market was not the same as the relational database market, and competing directly with a relational database meant that either the relational database company was in the wrong place or ODI was. If the problem could be solved with a relational database and the performance was satisfactory, then that is what they would buy regardless of the skill of the salesperson. When the value/resistance matrix from our earlier chapters is applied, the target market becomes very clear for an object database. The highest-value prospects would be those that would require and could justify the most run-time license fees. These would be the independent software vendors (ISVs), and they turned out to be the first large customers that ODI won.

The key requirement that the salespeople needed to determine once the opportunity was qualified, was how the companies were storing their data today. And the winning answer was that they needed to store their data in a proprietary file because it did not match what relational databases did. These proprietary files required a great deal of custom development and modification, which was not adding capability to their product. These ISVs wanted desperately to use a product that would allow them to store the application data and get access to it without having to develop additional software. So the ROI was simple: You are spending x on building your own storage technology today, and if you purchased ODI, you would spend less. This segment responded with high resistance because it was very competitive and required a great deal of prototyping to prove that the product would meet the prospect's requirements. They needed to be sure that ODI was the best match.

The use of the value/resistance matrix in Figure A.1 would have saved several careers at ODI and thousands of wasted hours chasing opportunities that just did not fit what the product could do or what people were willing to pay for.

AUGMENTING RELATIONAL DATABASES

The low-value/high-resistance quadrant turned out to be a trap for ODI. Relational databases were very good at managing information that fit into a table, much like a spreadsheet. Any information that did not fit into a table nicely or had complex relationships could fit into the relational model but was very slow to query. For example, suppose you are trying to determine

Value to the Seller

		High	Low
Resistance in Selling	High	Independent software vendors	Augmenting low performing relational applications
	Low	Proprietary flat file applications	Research and prototypes

Figure A.1 The value and resistance matrix.

relationships among people by the history of whom they talk to on the phone. The names and phone numbers fit great, but once you start trying to keep track of who is calling whom, it no longer is a nice fit. One solution is to use an object database, but all the reporting tools only work on relational databases. Another is to use an object database for the relationships of who is calling whom and a relational database for the table data. All the object databases companies fell into this trap and spent countless hours of time trying to make it work. All too often the prospect would give up on using two different technologies and just buy more powerful hardware to solve the performance problem.

RESEARCH AND PROTOTYPING

As in all early markets, there are the classic early adopters that like new products and will make small purchases. Companies like these early adopters because they represent some revenue and often they work for big-name companies. Unfortunately, although their purchases appear to be high value, they rarely are. ODI was no exception. It received several orders from technologists who simply wanted to play with the technology, but they barely generated any additional revenue. These sales were good for adding logos to the corporate presentation but not much else.

MARKET RESISTANCE

The ODI salespeople had to deal with large amounts of resistance in selling their database. This resistance was based on the complexity of storing software object structures in their actual form, as well as their interrelationships. These systems were highly technical, and the nature of the product was complex, requiring a great deal of technical hand-holding to build prototypes and to have them function well enough to prove that the product would meet the prospect's requirements. This prototyping process would sometimes take months and was almost always not funded, making it risky because if the technical resources were applied to one opportunity, they could not be applied to another.

HYPERCOMPETITIVE MARKET

All new products in a new market are competitive—and the object database market was as competitive as it gets. Each deal was critical because market share demonstrated leadership and prospects did not want to go with a company that would not be around in a few years. The prospects know that the market would only support a couple of venders and going with one of the losers would require having to swap the products out and repurchase. In cases where prospects were evaluating products, it was typical that while on a sales call the salesperson would see his or her competitor's names on the sign-in sheet in the lobby. It is in this market that setting and avoiding traps is required, as well as executing lockouts. Each of the competing companies was used to competition and was well trained in competitive issues.

SALES TRAINING

Like most companies, ODI implemented sales training that included several of the most popular and well-established sales methods available for complex business-to-business selling. What became obvious very quickly was that they were a great start but were completely insufficient to win this market. The training basically helped salespeople to come up with great questions and to identify the key players—but that was just the beginning. The training did not prepare the salespeople for the level of competition or the number of players involved in each deal. The salespeople needed to be the best prepared and the most aggressive if they were going to win this market. To break into new accounts that were not yet aware of object databases, the sales team needed skills to create the need and build a vision of how the prospects' world could be better by adopting object databases. If the salespeople positioned the product as a database, everyone would say, "We have already standardized on Oracle or Sybase." Without a creative way to build the vision, the sales team would be thought of a just another database. The best salespeople were able to quickly identify the key technical decision maker and build a vision of what their organization would be like if they did not have to build their own data storage but could simple plug one in.

THE FIRST CALL

The first sales call in selling ODI's object database was extremely important. As with most new technologies and disruptive products, there was a high level of curiosity within the marketplace. The early wins and the hype around object-oriented programming gave ODI a short window of opportunity that attracted high-level technologists. These first calls were a tight balance between building interest and digging to understanding how qualified the opportunity was. During these first calls, it was critical to set the traps that would lock out the competitors that would follow you at the account. The traps and lockouts were both technology- and business-oriented. An example of one of ODI's lockouts was a patented way in which the product accessed the objects in the database, which gave it the best performance of any product in the market. On the business or economic side, ODI had raised the most amount of capital, had the greatest number of customers, and had the largest field organization of engineers to support the implementation. Of course, the competitors had their own view on these lockout issues, as well as their own unique features and market segment successes.

THE TECHNICAL SALE

As mentioned, the technical sale required an enormous amount of on-site hand-holding, which included building a prototype or doing a head-to-head competitive proof of concept. The technical sale required engineers who had well-developed technical skills and who worked well with people. It was very consistent to see the most successful salespeople teamed with the most talented engineers. This also became one of the major issues in the growth of the company because the conventional model was to assign several salespeople to one engineer even when it was obvious that the inverse would have been more successful.

Often when a company is competing with sometimes three competitors, the technical sale would go to a competitor and the end run to the business players would have to be executed. Since the market was so early in its development, the requirements were not well established, and the technical people involved in the selection did not care about the business issues. Another common issue was that many of the salespeople were not technically knowledgeable enough to understand and argue the technical issues. The most common mistake during the technical sale was not getting an introduction to the project manager. Without this introduction, the salesperson was out in the cold if the technical sale was lost. Without starting the business sale early in the process, the salesperson was only doing half his or her job, and all too often, the competitor would pressure the project manager at the end of the quarter with a low bid contingent on moving forward immediately. Smart salespeople would use the first request for an evaluation copy as the perfect opportunity to request an introduction to the project manager, stating it was one of the requirements in the process.

THE BUSINESS SALE

The business sale had several levels of challenges, and if they were not started and addressed early in the process, the sale could be lost before the salesperson even realized it. Two opposing strategies could be used. The first was the baby-steps strategy, which in this case was to get a minimum purchase that would take the deal off the table, locking out competitors because the technical players would not want to explain that they purchased the wrong product and needed to purchase an additional product.

The second was the pull-it-forward strategy, which meant building up the costs of the run-time license fees in the future to show that a large prepayment would greatly reduce the long-term cost.

MAVERICK STRATEGIES

Moving Their Champion

Since the nature of object databases was highly complex and difficult to implement, the few who could do it well and make the product shine were in high demand. When placed into a target account, these talented few made the sales process a breeze. Because the champion was experienced with all the issues, the technical sale was a foregone conclusion. One of the salespeople at ODI befriended a small group of talented engineers, and once he finished a project at one customer, he would connect them with a new prospect. Of course, the prospect was always open-minded to hiring talented engineers, and the engineers were always interested a new challenge. This strategy was extremely powerful, and everyone wins. The strategy is a focused version of the ecosystems strategy, and with selling a complex product that is difficult to implement, having that resistance reduced is key to accelerating the sale.

The End Run

The end-run strategy was needed because the technical sale was a major gamble. The prospects evaluating the product did not have well-developed requirements, and they had their own agendas. Often the technical recommendation would be given based on misinformation or the first product that they reviewed. The nature of engineers is to work independently, and if they were not open to on-site help, there would be little chance to influence them. Also, the ODI product was not known for its ease of use; it was very powerful, but to exploit that power, you had to really dig in and get a strong understanding of how it worked. Not getting the technical recommendation happened so often that the salespeople were planning their end run from the first call. In fact, knowing the end-run strategy was so important that it became a hiring condition, and during the interviewing process, the master of the end run would give the candidate the case study and ask him or her, "So, what would you do?" The candidates who had not sold in highly competitive market spaces would not do well in this environment.

Refusing to Lose

This strategy is a slogan that became core to the sales culture at ODI. When losing was not an option, winning was the only alternative. At other companies people understand that there are alternatives to their product and that people will choose other products—but not at ODI. Anytime a deal was going south, the sales management would spring into action with an executive call to the prospect's leadership to explain that not going with ODI would be strategic mistake.

After each quarter there was a meeting at the home office to gain additional product training and begin planning for the next quarter's deals. It was clear that the company had found a niche that was being built into other companies' software products, and replacing a proprietary database and the run-time licenses fee was very advantageous to ODI because there would be future payments as the customer deployed its product. To most companies this would be considered a great market.

The key lesson here was that people were not replacing relational databases with ODI, which meant that it was not going to be a mainstream database but could capture a sizable and profitable niche. What kept the company from focusing on and exploiting this niche market was the belief that the next generation of database technology would be object-oriented in a way similar to how relational databases took over after hierarchical databases. This belief kept the investors excited and the employees thinking about what their stock options would be worth with an Oracle-like evaluation. It was this focus that kept the management from accepting why people would buy the product and what the company should do to get the next customer.

After a couple of years of missing the sales goals, the board explored the sale of the company. An offer was received for approximately $300 million, but it was thought too low and was rejected. The board of directors determined that changes were needed and that they needed to do a restart. The restart included a change in CEO and strategy. The new product strategy was to go after a completely new market where the company had no customers or experience.

HITTING THE WALL

In 1995 after rejecting a buyout offer, the company realized that object databases were not going to replace relational databases. Many of the original sales team had either moved into management or realized that their stock options were not enough to retire on and sought their fortunes elsewhere. After another year of missed expectations, the new CEO believed the problem was that the sales organization was not growing fast enough and that the company needed more "feet on the street."

A new VP of sales was recruited from a high-flying software company that had the reputation of a well-run sales organization. The new VP had only worked at one other software company before coming to ODI, and his previous company was the leader in its well-established market. So, it was no fault of his that he naturally wanted to run the team the only way he knew: Double the number of salespeople and add structure to the sales process. Quickly the company went on a hiring spree to fill the newly opened positions and established daily metrics of sales activity. The conventional model of taking a selling method that worked in an established market with an established product and apply it to a new product/new market seemed logical at the time, but it was disastrous in the end. It was a great deal like ignoring a recipe that required 30 minutes of cooking time in the oven at 350 degrees and thinking that if you turned the oven to 700 degrees, it would cook twice as fast. Of course, the quality of the salespeople had slipped greatly from the original team of mavericks to the current B- and C-players, which reduced the win rate and consumed corporate resources through lost opportunities.

In the end, the product did not become any easier to use, nor did the market grow at a greater rate. The new salespeople would follow the unproven process and report their metrics on timely bases, but the deals did not close. The pressure for revenue continued to increase, but the capability of generating that revenue was reduced because the remaining A-players' territory had shrunk to accommodate the new salespeople. This often-used approach to fix the sales growth problem cannot last long because soon the best people begin to leave more quickly than quality replacements can be hired.

Like most disruptive product companies that set their goal too high, once the key players wake from their dream and realize that the market for the product is a niche, it no longer excites them and they move on. Interestingly enough, the object database market is still alive and growing but is still just a niche market. Who knows what would have happened to ODI if it had focused on the high-value half of the quadrant and did not pull forward the run-time license fees?

RESTART AND RESTART AGAIN

Instead of exploiting the niche that accepted object databases, the team at ODI continued to apply the technology to the newest, hottest technology trend. After several restarts focusing on being a database for Web sites and later for XML documents, ODI, renamed Excelon, was low on cash and saw its revenues shrinking. It was sold for $24 million to Progress Software in 2003.

WHAT WAS LEARNED FROM THIS EXPERIENCE?

From a sales perspective, ODI's diverse group of salespeople, with very different approaches and styles, demonstrated that companies do not need to have a single sales process. The aggressiveness that was not pushy but laser-focused and intense, the competitiveness that literally "refused to lose," made competing against ODI extremely difficult. The flawless execution of the end run, left competitors wondering what happened and totally confused. Unlike the experience with Rational, where the focus was on determining the best way to sell the product and what organizational structure was needed to accomplish it, the salesperson at ODI had to take his or her skills and expectations to a whole new level.

ODI's key problem was more strategic than selling-related. The technical sale was so time-consuming that the ratio of engineers to salespeople was insufficient and should have been two engineers to every salesperson. The pulling forward of run-time licenses may have saved several weak quarters, but it stole future revenue and misrepresented the real growth rate of the company. The future revenue was not just the licenses that would eventually be brought in but also the gross value of the deal was greatly reduced. The incentives that were given to the customers to pay forward greatly reduced the gross value of the deal. It would have been interesting to see what would've happened if ODI focused on owning the object database niche and simply built off of that niche by making the product simpler to use, thereby reducing the resistance to adoption.

Endnotes

CHAPTER 1

1. Geoffrey A. Moore, *Crossing the Chasm: Marketing and Selling Disruptive Products to Mainstream Customers*, New York: HarperBusiness, 1991.

2. IBM originally beat out Hughes Aircraft in a hard-fought test-off competition in 1988, but the project cost has now grown by more than $1.5 billion and slipped nearly three years. Jack Robertson, "FAA, IBM Federal Plan to Fix Errant Air Traffic System," *Electronic News*, March 8, 1993.

3. "maverick." WordNet 3.0, Princeton University, July 31, 2008, http://dictionary.reference.com/browse/maverick.

4. Disruptive: The innovation that transforms the incumbent (e.g., the personal computer versus the mainframe, or missile weapons versus artillery, or downloadable digital media versus CDs and DVDs).

5. Revolutionary: The innovation that most often replaces the incumbent (e.g., the automobile versus the horse-drawn buggy, the printed word versus the manuscript, or semiconductors versus vacuum tubes).

6. Sustaining: The innovation that improves product performance of established products (e.g., Windows NT versus Windows XP or the aluminum baseball bat versus the wooden baseball bat). While sustaining technologies are often incremental, they can also be radical or discontinuous.

CHAPTER 4

1. Michel de Montaigne, trans. Donald M. Frame, *The Complete Essays of Montaigne*, "Of Glory," Stanford, CA: Stanford University, 1958, II:16, p. 473.

2. Alexis de Toqueville, *Democracy in America*, "How the Americans Combat Individualism by the Doctrine of Self-Interest Properly Understood," Penguin Classic, 2003, p. 524–525.

3. William Shakespeare, *Tragedy of Antony and Cleopatra*, Act II, Scene 5.

4. Sir Isaac Newton, *Philosophiae Naturalis Principia Mathematica* (1687).

Index

About the Authors

Brian G. Burns is a sales leader, advisor, and investor. He has spent his 20-year career creating, capturing, and dominating early-stage innovative markets. During this time, he has played key leadership, management, and sales roles for nine venture-capital-backed companies, resulting in three IPOs and six acquisitions. Through this experience, he has developed a unique and powerful sales method for bringing innovative products to market while marginalizing competitors. In his private practice, Brian has founded The Maverick Organization, a consulting firm specializing in assisting companies with their sales strategy and sales practices and in developing an effective sales team.

Thomas U. Snyder received his BS and MBA from the University of Maryland. Tom began his career by joining the United States federal government where he held a variety of analyst positions, most prominently as a member of the White House staff under two different presidents. After eight years in federal service, Tom left to start his first company. Over the course of the next 15 years, Tom started, developed, and sold a series of successful enterprises. Being a serial entrepreneur and a long-time student of the science of sales, Tom was drawn to leveraging his sales and entrepreneurial expertise to help both large and small enterprises improve sales performance. To that end, he joined the firm Huthwaite, Inc., where he served in two different positions over 10 years: Senior Vice President of Research, Product Development and Sales Strategy and CEO. As the company's lead consultant, Tom advised C-level executives at more than 100 of the Fortune 500.

Tom coauthored *Escaping the Price-Driven Sale* in 2007. Currently in private practice, Tom consults with companies of all sizes in the areas of revenue growth, market penetration, sales strategy, sales skills, and sales process by employing strategic thinking, entrepreneurial zeal, business development skills, diagnostic experience, and sales force development expertise. Tom was named the *2005 Entrepreneur of the Year* by the Corporate Finance Institute of Washington, D.C., and in January of 2008 he was named one of America's 100 Most Influential Sales Leaders by the editors of the *Encyclopedia of Selling*. He is a nationally known speaker who delivers more than 50 speeches to salespeople and sales leaders across the globe each year.